The *Decline* and *Revival* of the British Passenger Fleet

The Elders and Fyffes' passenger cargo liner *Camito* (1956) heading down Southampton Water.

Nick Robins

6 5 4 3 2 1

© N S Robins and Colourpoint Books
Newtownards 2001

Designed by Colourpoint Books,
Newtownards
Printed by Nicholson & Bass Ltd

ISBN 1 898392 69 2

Colourpoint Books
Unit D5, Ards Business Centre
Jubilee Road
NEWTOWNARDS
County Down
Northern Ireland
BT23 4YH
Tel: (028) 9182 0505
Fax: (028) 9182 1900
E-mail: Info@colourpoint.co.uk
Web-site: www.colourpoint.co.uk

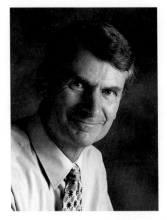

Although employed as a chartered geologist, Dr Nick Robins maintains a long-standing passion for the sea and its shipping. Interest has concentrated on British and Irish flag short-sea routes as well as the deep-sea liner services operated under the Red Ensign. A keen shipping photographer, he began by photographing ships on the Manchester Ship Canal in 1960, but quickly progressed to include all the major British and Irish passenger carriers that have seen service since the mid-1960s. His photographs have appeared in numerous magazines and books. Nick Robins is also the author of a number of articles for *Sea Breezes* and other journals, and of several books. He is married with four children.

By the same author:
The Evolution of the British Ferry
The British Excursion Ship
Turbine Steamers of the British Isles

Photo Credits
All photographs in this book have been taken by the author, Nick Robins, unless otherwise stated.

Cover Photographs
Front cover: The *Southern Cross*, *Carmania* and *Franconia* laid up at Southampton in May 1972.
Henry Gunston
Back cover: The *St Helena* (1990) at Capetown.
Henry Gunston

Contents

Preface

In 1960 there were 115 British registered ships with berths for 50 or more passengers. These ranged from the mighty Cunard liners which maintained the North Atlantic ferry routes, to the diminutive *Mombasa* which operated the British India Line's East African coastal services. Britain was at the centre of a web of passenger routes, nearly all of which converged on either London, Liverpool or Southampton. There were also a number of services in the Indian Ocean which serviced the needs of the ailing British Empire.

This fleet rapidly halved in numbers over the next ten years. By 1980 there were only 13 British registered passenger or cruise ships. There were many reasons for this decline, not least the arrival of the jet airliner, but rising fuel costs, the onset of containerised cargo handling and industrial unrest also contributed. Salvation arrived with the burgeoning cruise ship industry. By 2001 there will be 16 ocean-going British passenger ships, numbers boosted in 2000 by the transfer of most of the Princess Cruises fleet from the Liberian registry to UK.

This book traces the demise and modest revival of the British fleet, between 1960 and 2000, within its proper historical context. It records the career highlights of each of the ships and describes the features characteristic of each vessel and its owners. The book describes how the 'baronial hall'- type internal décor, along with the distinctive hacienda-like decorations aboard the old *Reina del Pacifico*, were displaced in the 1930s with the arrival of the Orient Line's *Orion* with her spacious, light and airy public rooms. The subsequent need to replace the war-torn fleet then put design and innovation to one side, until the *Southern Cross*, the *Oriana* and the *Canberra* were conceived. Subsequent design for the cruise market is for larger and larger ships with big internal spaces and light pastel décor. Brick fireplaces in smoking rooms and wood panelled dining saloons are now a thing of the past.

Technology has also advanced. The steam turbine engine was succeeded by the diesel, and this in turn is now being displaced by diesel-electric systems. Lighter construction techniques and propellers mounted on directional pods will allow modern ships to berth without assistance in shallow and confined harbours attractive to the cruise passenger.

I must thank a number of people and organisations who have helped with the preparation of this book. I am most grateful for the critical review of the manuscript carried out by my colleague Henry Gunston. Permission to borrow and use artifacts and photographs has been freely given by John Shepherd, John Sutton, Ellie and Darren Everhart, Henry Gunston and others, and I have enjoyed the full cooperation of the Peninsular & Oriental Steam Navigation Company, Princess Cruises and FotoFlite. I thank all of you and hope that you enjoy the finished product.

Nick Robins
Crowmarsh
Oxfordshire
September 2001

1. A Fabulous Heritage

The romantic film *Titanic*, released in 1998, exploits nostalgia for the days of the great Atlantic liners. Forgotten is the discomfort of travel in steerage class; forgotten also is the need to leave home to try one's luck in a new continent – the romantic ideal of travel on a great liner, albeit one that the film maker reconstructed over a period of two years at 90% actual scale, is overwhelming. Liner passengers enjoyed a camaraderie, even in steerage, which reflected the temporary, but synthetic, social structure of life aboard a main line passenger ship, where 2,000 people could be thrown together for between one and anything up to six weeks.

The love stories tend to gloss over what happened to the passengers when their ship finally docked at the foreign port and their life began anew. Arrival at port, and disembarkation from that last piece of Britain can be an emotional moment, with the realisation that a new life starts and a new country beckons. Farewells to fellow passengers are hard, but life over the next few years may be even harder. That being so, the social delights of life at sea are undeniable, and it is exactly this that has helped develop the new cruising industry over the last 30 years. Today the cruise ship takes a prominent position in the travel agent's window, and investment in new passenger tonnage continues at a remarkable high.

The romantic literature also overlooks the bitter rivalry between operators, particularly on the North Atlantic. When Leyland, Dominion and White Star were bought up by the American Shipping Combine, set up in 1902 with capital assets of £24 million, Cunard nervously went cap in hand to the British government for assistance in order to maintain its fleet. In return, they were instructed to respond to the behest of the Admiralty should they be so required. It is often overlooked that the mighty *Titanic*, although registered in Liverpool, was actually American owned, under the chairmanship of Mr Ismay. Later, in 1934, amalgamation of Cunard and White Star was enforced by the British government as a condition of further grant aid, this time for the construction of the *Queen Mary*.

With her paying-off pennant flying in the drizzle, the *Queen Mary* (1936) leaves Southampton on her final voyage – to Long Beach, California – on 31 October 1967.

Seen at Long Beach in 1998, the excellent state of preservation of the *Queen Mary* is evident from the view aft from the bridge wings.

Ellie Everhart

The bridge controls aboard the *Queen Mary*, complete with descriptive plaques.

Ellie Everhart

The *Caronia* (1948) returns to Southampton from a cruise in August 1965.

The 50 years between 1950 and 2000 have seen a complete cycle of development. The early post-war redevelopment programme encouraged 1930s' designs to be constructed well into the 1950s, with inefficient and outdated turbine machinery, cramped and ill-ventilated accommodation, and stuffy public rooms very much the vogue. Innovation only became apparent in the mid-1950s, when the Pametrada turbine provided new levels of mechanical efficiency. Even in 1960 the mistaken perception that the diesel engine could never produce enough power to sustain a big passenger liner was still being published. Increased demand for passenger comfort drove improved interior design requirements. Cunard's new *Caronia*, built in 1948, actually provided private en suite facilities in every cabin, an item which endeared the ship to many of the more affluent post-war travellers. At that time the need to transport people between continents by sea was maintained at record levels.

In the post-war years only tourist class and first class accommodation were generally offered on the North Atlantic. Cabin class had become an intermediate grade rather than the best a ship could offer. The tourist class concept was pioneered by P&O, with their five 1930s-built *Strath*-class liners (see Appendix 1). But on the North Atlantic in post-war years, most tourist class ships, such as Cunard's *Saxonia* and her three sisters, were equipped with a few first class berths so that a lower and more competitive tourist class fare could be realised, in line with the rules of the North Atlantic Passenger Conference. Exceptions to this were the all-first class ships *Media* and *Parthia*, although their first class accommodation was more akin to second class on the *Queen Elizabeth*, except that many of the cabins were larger.

On the Pacific and Far Eastern services tourist class remained dominant, due to the sustained level of emigration to Australia and New Zealand.

8 July 1934. The nearly complete *Strathnaver* (1931) is pulled off the fitting-out quay at Barrow to allow the newly launched *Strathaird* (1932) alongside.   *The Sankey Collection*

The *Oriana* (1960), last of the Orient Line ships, was built for high capacity, long distance liner voyages.

P&O's *Strathnaver* and *Strathaird* had both become tourist class only ships and, of course, the Shaw Savill Line's *Southern Cross* and *Northern Star* were tourist class ships. For the most part, other P&O and Orient Line ships offered first and tourist class and the Union Castle mail-ships were also two class.

Although notable ship design of this era includes the *Reina del Mar*, the *Southern Cross* and the *Windsor Castle*, there was no significant landmark in British liner design until the *Oriana* and the *Canberra* came to the fore in the early 1960s. In the meantime, of course, there were some wonderful ships built and commissioned for a variety of owners, on diverse routes with diverse operating requirements. Beauty, of course, is subjective, but the Elder Dempster liner *Aureol* must be a candidate for the finest, and conversely Cunard's *Media* and *Parthia*, both originally laid down as Brocklebank Line freighters, must be the plainest.

In the immediate post-war years those liners that could be refurbished and put back into service presented, for the most part, an austere picture. Few new ships had been built in the depressed years of the 1930s and many of these newer ships had in any case been lost to the ravages of war. Notable survivors included the Queens and the *Mauretania*, as well as the Royal Mail Line's new first class only *Andes* and four of P&O's five *Strath*-class ships. The *Strathallan* had been lost in the invasion of North Africa in 1942, while serving alongside her four sisters and three other P&O liners. Most liner companies were faced with an urgent need to rebuild their fleets in anticipation of renewed international commercial development. Hindered by post-war materials shortages, inflated shipbuilding costs, as well as temporary bans on international travel, few of these operators could have foreseen that within a few decades the ubiquitous Boeing 747 would overtake them. In the meantime, competition to restore the post-war liner routes to their former glory was intense.

In 1939, the *Queen Mary* held the prestigious Blue Riband, and the British passenger fleet was internationally respected. After the war the fleet was smaller, and it never quite managed to regain its premiership. There were some fine rebuffs to this trend: the new combination transatlantic ferry and cruise ship *Caronia*, for example, was designed to say that the Red Ensign meant quality – provided you, the customer, could afford it!

Just as the Anchor Line had built bigger and better ships for the emigrant service from Scotland to North America after that trade had peaked in the 1920s, so Cunard and Canadian Pacific built ships to nurture this declining exodus in the 1950s. But worse, both P&O and the Orient Line pinned their future on the emigrant business, and a series of unimaginative post-war builds flooded the round-the-world service until it was realised that saturation and a declining market were commercially dangerous. A more competitive market was rapidly developing with, among others, Greek shipowners, who enjoyed lower overheads, soon joining the fray. Other new passenger ship operating countries included Egypt, Yugoslavia, Israel and Turkey. But in true British style, the changing nature of both the market and of the competition were ignored for too long.

Cunard again went to the government for a soft loan, this time for £20 million, to build the *QE2*. A series of company mergers indicated that times were indeed hard. Typical of these was the conjunction of the Peninsular & Oriental Steam Navigation Company and the Orient Steam Navigation Company in 1960, although both companies kept their own separate identity for some years.

In the early 1960s, Union Castle (who had merged with Clan Line in 1955) finally managed to upgrade the speed of their liner service to South Africa, with the delivery of the *Windsor Castle* and the *Transvaal Castle*. This allowed an eleven and a half day service to Capetown at 22½ knots. These ships respectively replaced the *Winchester Castle*, dating from 1930, and the *Carnarvon Castle*, which had entered service in 1926. Back in 1957 the company had upgraded the specification for

The *Edinburgh Castle* (1948) off the New Docks at Southampton in June 1969.

the *Pendennis Castle*, including lengthening the ship even while she lay on the stocks, to ensure that she would also be able to maintain the new speed. The earlier sisters *Edinburgh Castle* and *Pretoria Castle* were already capable of 22½ knots.

But the reality was that the majority of liner operators found that they were holding an asset they could no longer afford. Within only two years of the establishment of the upgraded service, the long awaited dream of the Union Castle Line was in decline and this magnificent service was soon to be no more. The Union Castle experience was not unique, and a number of other well known liner operators disappeared quietly without trace from the stock exchange listings at that time.

The heritage of all these companies was second to none. On the Atlantic, the *United States* had taken the record for the fastest crossing between the Ambrose Light and Bishop Rock, with an average of 35.6 knots. The previous best of the *Queen Mary* was only 31.7 knots. In turn, she had wrestled the award from the French liner *Normandie* in 1936 and again in 1938, as the two ships worked up their speed in their early careers. Prior to that, the Italian *Rex* and the German liners

Bremen and *Europa* had fought with the British *Mauretania* and *Lusitania* for the recognised speed. On a fast Atlantic crossing the old *Mauretania* could maintain over 27 knots, and she was logged at a speed of 29.8 knots for the 170 kilometre crossing between Plymouth and Cherbourg in 1929.

Each of the colonial powers developed their own fleet of passenger ships to service their own territories and French, German, Italian and Spanish passenger ships competed for fares on diverse routes, accommodating as best they could, the dual requirements of passenger and cargo. As a consequence, there was a clear divide between the main line passenger services of the North Atlantic and the passenger and cargo demands on many of the South American routes, where passengers were subject to delays and altered schedules according to the needs of cargo handling at each port.

As the passenger demand declined on the traditional routes, many of the liner companies increasingly put their ships to cruising, particularly during off season periods. Cruising had been used to generate income during the depressed years of the 1930s, when ships such as Ellerman's *City of*

Nagpur, inward bound to North Sea ports in the autumn, carried out short duration cruises to the Baltic before resuming liner voyages, and also undertook occasional or seasonal cruises based on Southampton. The British-flagged Furness Bermuda Line (Furness Withy) New York to Bermuda 'booze cruise', with casino and sex shop, had been inaugurated as far back as 1919, but the service only survived until 1966, falling foul of stringent US safety laws. The demand for more exotic cruising was stimulated by the *Caronia* when she was put into the American market on a seasonal basis in 1949, and this demand slowly grew to become a rapidly developing industry through the 1980s and 1990s.

A notable success story is that of Princess Cruises. Developed by Seattle interests in the 1960s, with the Canadian Pacific Railways' steamer *Princess Patricia* on their Alaskan service, it soon blossomed using the charter market to include Panama Canal and Caribbean routes. In 1974 it was acquired by P&O and the fleet was made up with the *Sun Princess*, built for P&O only

in 1972 as the *Spirit of London*, and two equally young former Norwegian-owned cruise ships which became the *Pacific Princess* and the *Island Princess*. A key to advertising the new fleet was the contemporary television series *The Love Boat*, which was developed for an American audience and set aboard the *Island Princess*. Much like the film *Titanic*, these programmes concentrated on the romantic goings on of both passengers and crew and made full use of the exotic cruise destinations. Today, much of the fleet remains British and Italian crewed, reflecting the take-over of the Italian-owned Sitmar Cruises in 1988.

But what of that wonderful liner heritage personified by Cunard, P&O, British India, Royal Mail, Pacific Steam and those other traditional liner companies? In addition to these main line services, there were also numerous lesser routes offered by, for example, the Anchor Line, Henderson Line and the Booth Line out of Liverpool; the New Zealand Line, Blue Star Line and Ellerman & Bucknall out of London; as well as the secondary routes on offer by British India

The Ellerman Line's *City of Nagpur* (1922) was deployed on North Sea cruises by the Wilson Line between liner voyages in the 1930s. She was the victim of a submarine attack in April 1941.   *J & M Clarkson Collection*

WILSON LINE.

R.M.S. "City of Nagpur."

Programme of Music.

FAREWELL DINNER.

Signature Tune	City of Nagpur March		*Harper*
1 Waltz	The Blue Danube		*Strauss*
2 Potpourri	A Musical Jig-saw		*Aston*
3 Intermezzo	Moon Madrigal		*Willeby*
4 Selection	The Pink Lady		*Caryll*
5 Two Pieces	Sizilietta / Diokon o' Devon		*von Blon* / *Holliday*
6 Suite	Woodland Pictures		*Fletcher*
7 Medley	50 Years of Song		*Baynes*
Signature Tune			

Mixed Fruit Cocktail
Hors d'œuvres
Consommé Printanier—Potage Marie Stuart
Boiled Scotch Salmon—Balmoral
Lamb Cutlets—Green Peas
To order—Kidney Omelettes
Roast Sirloin Beef—Yorkshire Pudding—Horseradish Sauce
Braised Turkey and Sausage—Cranberry Sauce
Browned and Boiled Potatoes
French Beans   Dressed Cabbage
Asparagus Vinaigrette
(Cold) Braised York Ham   Corned Ox Tongue   Chicken Roll
Salad
Parisienne Trifle   Jelly à la Russe
Tutti-frutti Ices
Cheese—Cheddar   Edam   Stilton   Kraft
Oatcakes   Biscuits   Cheese Straws
Fresh Fruit
Dessert   Coffee

Thursday, 9th July, 1936.

The cruise dinner menu for 9 July 1936 from the *City of Nagpur*.

and Union Castle. There also remained a number of troop transports that were still in service and some of these were later to offer exciting potential for the development of the school ship cruise idea.

Appendix 2 lists those vessels which were in service in 1960. It illustrates the large number and diversity of passenger ships that were in service at that time. Not listed are the smaller carriers capable of carrying up to 30 first class passengers (see Appendix 1).

The year 1960 was a memorable one: the *Canberra* was launched on 16 March and the maiden voyage of the *Oriana* commenced on 3 December. The *Empress of Canada*, *Transvaal Castle*, *Northern Star*, and of course the *Queen Elizabeth 2* were all yet to be commissioned. There were 115 ships certified to carry over 50 passengers to foreign shores; their average age was 15 years and the aggregate gross tonnage was two million. Although the liner trade was suffering from declining patronage and rising costs, it was still a

thriving industry. Turn-around times had been reduced, staffing efficiencies had been introduced and profits, for the most part small profits, were still being made.

There remained a belief that the aeroplane would only affect the larger passenger units and that the smaller passenger carriers would survive untouched. Even in the late 1950s, the 'board room' tended to view air travel as a fad and was convinced that most travellers would continue to patronise the liner routes. But even in 1959, 1.5 million passengers crossed the Atlantic by air and only 0.9 million went by sea. The industry was facing complete change, and the story that has evolved since is one of almost terminal decline, at a rate of five ships per year until the late 1970s (Figure 1, opposite). The reasons behind the decline were many and compelling. There were five principal factors which conspired towards massively reduced profits and vessel re-routing at a very critical time: competition from the air;

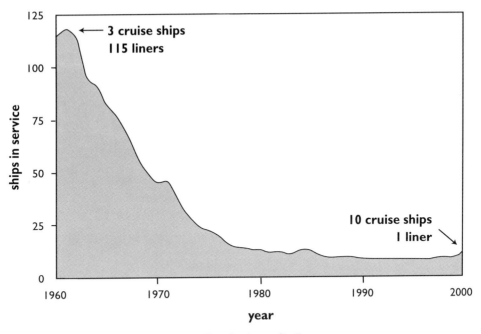

Figure 1: Number of Passenger Ships in Service (See also Appendix 1)

The *Grand Princess* (1998), one of five ships re-flagged to the UK by Princess Cruises in 2000.

Princess Cruises

The *Empress of Canada* (1961) moving up the River Mersey towards the Princes Landing Stage in August 1967.

spiralling costs of fuel; ever stricter maritime safety rules, particularly in the United States; the onset of containerisation with liners equipped to handle general cargo only; the National Seaman's Union strike of 1966, the dock strike of 1967 and the prolonged closure of the Suez Canal from June 1967, for the second time in a decade.

Competition from the air had a dramatic effect on transatlantic sea passenger numbers. In 1957 the number peaked, even higher than the all-time great figures of 1913, but the decline thereafter was rapid:

1957	1,036,000
1965	642,000
1969	332,000
1971	25,000

The economies of fuel consumption and energy saving that the shipowners earnestly sought throughout the 1970s became the envy of the airlines in the early 1980s. In 1982 alone, Laker Airways, Braniff International and World Airways all went out of business and the airline industry found itself badly in debt, as passengers demanded cheaper and more accessible travel. The lessons learnt earlier by the shipping industry were now being taken up in earnest by the airlines.

In due course, the passenger shipping industry received a life-saving injection as cruising began to exploit a nucleus market. This has now developed into a new, relatively small but profitable business under the Red Ensign, ironically by using the aeroplane as a common means of getting to and from the cruise ship. At the beginning of the year 2000 there were just ten cruise ships and one cargo-passenger liner registered in Britain (cf only three dedicated cruise ships in 1960); the average age of the 11 ships was ten years and the aggregate gross tonnage was only 0.4 million. This amounted to only 10% of the number of ships and 20% of the tonnage available in 1960. During 2000, Princess Cruises re-flagged five of its Liberian-registered cruise ships to the Red Ensign in response to UK tax concessions. This provided a much needed boost to the British merchant fleet, doubling the aggregate tonnage to 0.8 million. Princess Cruises' President Peter Ratcliffe said: "The British flag has had a long and proud seafaring tradition, and it also represents some of the highest operating standards in the world. Princess has long met the highly regarded operating requirements of the UK flag and it seems sensible for us now to move our fleet to the British registry".

This is the story of the demise of the traditional markets between 1960 and 2000. It is also the story of the development of the cruise ship, with eight more cruise ships on order for anticipated delivery to UK registry by 2004.

Right: The Michelangelo Dining Room aboard the *Grand Princess* (1998). Contrast this with the interior of the *Viceroy of India* (1929) below.
Princess Cruises

Below: P&O's innovative turbo-electric driven *Viceroy of India* (1929) was decorated in traditional baronial hall style – this is the first class smoking room. The ship was lost in the war.
P&O Steam Navigation Company

2. Mainline Services to the Americas

The mainline transatlantic ships need little introduction here. The flagships were undoubtedly the Queens. They were essentially of the 1920s design era, built to a grand and impressive theme during the 1930s. Refurbished after the war years, they had already become yesterday's ships by the beginning of the 1960s. Principal competitors on the New York run were then the *United States* and the *France*, and both offered far more advanced features for creature comfort than could the Queens. However, the two grand old ladies continued to thrive in a declining market, using the momentum of their own majesty to maintain passenger numbers.

The life of the Queens had not been easy. The *Queen Mary* was laid down in December 1930, during the first year of the Great Depression. Passenger numbers had fallen by nearly a half in two years and in December 1931 Cunard called a

halt to building, before going to the government for a £3 million loan. The new ship was only completed in 1936, when she promptly recovered the coveted Blue Riband from the French liner *Normandie*. Although the *Normandie* stole the prize back again in 1937, the *Queen Mary* recaptured it the following year and held it until the new American liner *United States* took it away from her again 14 years later.

Work started on the construction of the *Queen Elizabeth* with a further 'soft' loan of £5 million, conditional on amalgamation of Cunard with White Star. The maiden voyage of the *Queen Elizabeth* was scheduled for April 1940. In the event, the unfinished ship was dispatched away from hostilities to lay-up in New York during March 1940, then on to Singapore in the autumn to be fitted out for war service. Both the *Queens* spent the war years on troopship duties, carrying

The *Queen Mary* (1936) seen alongside the Southampton Ocean Terminal in July 1964.

A routine departure from Southampton to New York for the *Queen Elizabeth* (1940) in October 1968.

up to 15,000 men at a time. There was one major incident when, in October 1942, the *Queen Mary* collided with her escort, the cruiser HMS *Curacoa*, and sank her with the loss of 338 men.

There was always a regret on Merseyside that neither ship ever visited Liverpool, which was their port of registry. The Gladstone Dock could have accommodated them against the West Wall, although they could not have turned in the dock. The *Queen Mary* was rostered to sail to Australia from Gladstone Dock (named after a former chairman of the Mersey Docks and Harbour Board, not after the nineteenth century prime minister!) in 1942, but it was the *Mauretania* and the old *Aquitania* which actually arrived in port to take the voyage.

In post-war years the two Queens maintained the weekly service between Southampton, Cherbourg and New York, using the specially built Ocean Terminal at Southampton. The two ships were often booked up well in advance. The 1939-built *Mauretania* provided a secondary and slower summer-only service with Le Havre and Cobh as the intermediate calls. The *Mauretania*

was designed for the London to New York route. Built at Birkenhead by Cammell Laird, she was launched in July 1938, taking just 50 seconds from the moment she started to move until she slid off the way ends into the Mersey. Surprisingly larger than her former namesake (1907–35) by nearly 6,000 tons gross, she was actually 5 m shorter in length but broader in the beam by 0.5 m. As built, she could carry 486 cabin class, 390 tourist and 502 third class passengers and she needed a crew of 594. She was particularly well appointed; notable were the cabin class Grand Hall and the tourist class saloon, smoking room and lounge. Each class had its own cinema. Her maiden voyage was from Liverpool, returning to London, when she became the largest ship ever to enter the King George V Dock. After her third voyage she moved to New York, before being requisitioned as a troop transport.

After the war the *Mauretania* was refurbished by her builders and emerged early in 1947 with restyled accommodation for 475 first, 390 second and 304 third class passengers. Her subsequent career was spent on liner voyages and there was an increasing emphasis on cruising (see Chapter 8). She completed her liner career in 1965, with eight transatlantic voyages and a cruise to the Black Sea before sailing to the ship breakers.

Passenger numbers on the transatlantic sea routes quickly declined at the expense of air travel. By 1957, numbers were back at the same level as they had been in 1929. But in the autumn of 1958 the first commercial jet airliner service commenced between London and the United States, and in the eight years prior to 1965 sea passage numbers declined by a further 30%. Only one sixth of the passenger traffic on offer then crossed the Atlantic by sea. Sir John Brocklebank, speaking as Cunard's chairman at a press conference in October 1961, said:

> The company has decided to postpone, for the time being, placing an order for a replacement for the *Queen Mary*. Since the plan to build a 75,000 ton liner had been originated in 1959, the North Atlantic passenger liner trade had become less remunerative. Among the factors which had adversely affected the company's earnings was a tendency for the potential first class passenger across the North Atlantic to use air travel to an increasing extent. Passenger numbers on the Queens have fallen sharply enough to prompt new thinking about the two ship service. Five years ago they carried 126,000 passengers. The numbers dropped to 118,000 by 1959, to 111,000 in 1960, and would be about 100,000 in 1961.

Not surprisingly, the *Queen Elizabeth* and *Queen Mary* took up winter cruising, as the air lines now provided the unprofitable off-season service between UK and America. Inevitably, in 1967, the *Queen Mary* was withdrawn, leaving her consort the *Queen Elizabeth* to carry on alone.

The *Queen Mary* had carried over two million passengers and had steamed six million kilometres. Today she remains a stationary exhibit at Long Beach in California, having originally been sold to the city for $3.45 million. In her static role she has had various owners and lessees, but remains a financial success as a theme attraction, hotel and conference venue to this day. Her final voyage was sold as a 39-day cruise, leaving Southampton on 31 October 1967, round Cape Horn and eventually up the Pacific coast to Long Beach. Apparently the voyage through the tropics was somewhat trying, as the old ship and her cruise passengers sweated together. Indeed, she nearly did not sail at all, as the crew held a quayside strike on the eve of her departure to demand an increase in the traditional Cunard cruising bonus of £5 to £40.

The original design for the 75,000 ton replacement for the *Queen Mary* was much along the lines of the *France*, with accommodation in three classes. This idea was finally dropped after tenders for construction had actually been issued in 1963. The redesigned replacement was laid down in July 1965; a smaller ship (Appendix 3), built with the dual role of transatlantic liner and cruise ship, the *QE2* was nevertheless capable of over 30 knots as built (see Chapter 10).

The old *Queen Elizabeth* received a major refit over the winter of 1965–66 and this was intended to place her as a partner to the new ship. As it was, the new *Queen Elizabeth 2* began her maiden voyage on 2 May 1969 and the *Queen Elizabeth* was retired immediately and sold. She was taken to Fort Lauderdale and under the new name *The Queen*, was to be developed as a conference centre and hotel. This plan failed and she was bought at auction for $3.2 million for conversion to an education ship for CY Tung's Island Navigation Corporation. In January 1972, with the $11 million refit of the *Queen Elizabeth* almost complete, and now renamed *Seawise University*, she caught fire and sank in Hong Kong harbour. Ironically, this was a location not that remote from where she was originally fitted out as a troopship.

Happily, the *Queen Elizabeth 2* is still in service. Her original steam turbine machinery was always difficult, and with 1,600 passengers on board, her boilers failed in April 1974 on a cruise from New

The *Queen Elizabeth 2* (1968) in her original livery at Southampton in May 1969.

York to the Caribbean; the media thought this was wonderful! However, she made up for this the following year when she reportedly made a profit of £1 million on her 1975 world cruise. She was requisitioned for service as a troopship for the Falklands War in 1982 (Chapter 10), but even then her engines were causing problems. A staged farewell from the Defence Minister and senior military officers at Southampton was completed to schedule under the spotlight of the world's media. But maintenance on two of her boilers remained to be dealt with, and she sailed away from the fanfare to anchor quietly off the Isle of Wight while the outstanding work was put in hand. Only then did she sail south to war.

The *Queen Elizabeth 2* forsook her troublesome turbine engines for diesel-electric drive in the winter of 1986–87. The work was carried out by Lloyd-Werft at Bremerhaven at a cost of £100 million, all possible British contenders withdrawing from the bidding process for this extensive programme of work. On return to duty, the *Queen Elizabeth 2* quickly attracted a reputation as the world's greatest cruise ship. She

has since received a number of major refits, the last valued at £12 million reducing her passenger capacity from 1,750 to 1,500 and allowing the ship to be brought into line with the latest SOLAS requirements. Over £300 million has been spent on upgrading the ship since she was built at a cost of only £29 million in 1967. Today she continues to visit Southampton, her home port, to remind the city of the great days of the Ocean Terminal and of transatlantic voyages. In those days there was an express departure for New York every week, and the *Mauretania* visited every second week. In addition, there was also a departure, two weeks out of every three, for Le Havre and Cobh (occasionally also Rotterdam) to Montreal and Quebec during summer months and New York and Halifax in the winter.

As a one class ship the 'C' passengers on the *Queen Elizabeth 2* use the Caronia Restaurant on the Upper Deck; 'P' passengers, the Princess and Britannia Grills; and 'Q' passengers, the Queen's Grill. All 1,500 passengers can now be served at a single sitting. Bars include the famous Golden Lion, the Chart Room, which contains a piano

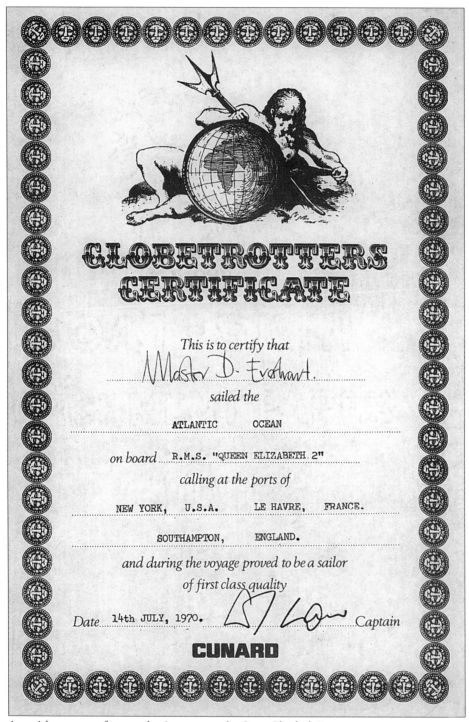

A special memento of a transatlantic voyage on the *Queen Elizabeth 2*.

The *Carinthia* (1956) in the River Mersey in September 1966.

from the *Queen Mary*, and the Crystal Bar. Younger passengers are entertained in the Club 2000. The officers and some of the crew are British, but many of the 'hotel' staff, including stewards, as well as deck and engineering crew, are Filipino. Some 320 members of the crew are female.

The Canadian route was served by the *Saxonia* and *Ivernia*, built in 1954 and 1955 respectively. Until 1961, London was the terminal port, but thereafter it became Southampton. This pair of ships was the first of a quartet, the younger sisters *Carinthia* and *Sylvania* being stationed at Liverpool – also on the Canadian service – until the *Sylvania* was switched to take over the Liverpool–Cobh–New York run on the retirement of the elderly *Britannic* in 1961.

The *Britannic*, sister to the slightly younger *Georgic*, had been built for the White Star Line in 1930 for the Liverpool to New York service, with a dual role as a cruise ship. At the time she was the largest motor ship under the Red Ensign, and internationally second only in size to the Italian liner *Augustus*. The *Georgic* was largely used on the

government-assisted emigrant service to Australia in post war years and was sold to shipbreakers in 1955 (Chapter 3).

The four new *Saxonia*-class ships for the Canadian service each had a gross tonnage of 21,650 and a service speed of 19 knots. Externally they were almost identical, but each ship had its own distinctive décor inside. As built, they could accommodate 125 first class and 800 tourist class passengers and they also had substantial cargo capacity. However, by 1963 Cunard were looking for other means of employing the Southampton-based pair and they were dispatched for a major refit to become dual purpose liners and cruise ships. For this role they were given lime green hulls similar to the *Caronia*, the company's main cruise liner, and in keeping with their new image were renamed: the *Saxonia* became the *Carmania* and the *Ivernia* was given the name *Franconia*.

The *Sylvania* undertook the first post-war Cunard cruise out of the Mersey in February 1965. In 1967 the *Sylvania*, *Carmania* and *Franconia* were all painted white, only the *Carinthia* retaining her original black hull. In

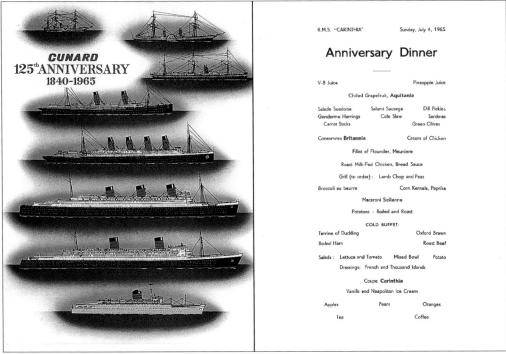

The dinner menu for 4 July 1965 from the *Carinthia*.

October the *Carinthia* made two round trips to Montreal from Southampton and was laid up awaiting disposal, being joined by the *Sylvania* in April 1968. The Canadian service was then abandoned and the *Carmania* and *Franconia* were solely devoted to cruising (see Chapter 8).

Even the old *Mauretania* was restyled and given the new cruise ship livery in 1962, and she then spent a large part of each year on cruises, mainly to the Mediterranean. Although based briefly at London before the war, she was always a Southampton ship in post-war years. In the early 1960s, as much as eight months of the year was spent on cruising, but in the early autumn of 1965 she was finally destored and sent to Inverkeithing for demolition. It was a premature end for a fine ship whose career was overshadowed by her big sisters. As a final insult, the Ocean Terminal, completed for the Queens only in 1950, was demolished in 1983 to make space for storing imported cars.

At Liverpool, Canadian Pacific was also facing problems. They took delivery of the *Empress of Canada* in 1961 and she commenced her maiden voyage from Liverpool in April 1961, under the command of Captain JP Dobson. To the accompaniment of patriotic Canadian music, the new ship edged away from Princes Landing Stage in the evening sunlight, dressed overall. It was an event that was recorded on live television. She joined the older sisters *Empress of England* and *Empress of Britain*, and was essentially of similar design. However, it was quickly obvious that a three ship service to Canada could not be maintained throughout the year, due to a fall off in the Canadian emigrant traffic and the arrival of the aeroplane. The older pair – *Empress of Britain* and *Empress of England* – which dated from 1956 and 1957 respectively, spent an increasing amount of the year chartered out to cruising organisations, working out of both Liverpool and Southampton as well as Capetown.

The *Sylvania* (1957) in the all-white hull colour adopted in later years, seen at Southampton in October 1967.

The *Empress of Britain* (1956) in Gladstone Dock at Liverpool in September 1964.

The *Empress of England* (1957) seen in the Mersey in May 1964.

The *Empress of England* (1957) seen in the Mersey carrying the new Canadian Pacific livery, July 1969.

The *Empress of Britain* left the fleet in 1965 to join the Greek Line as the *Queen Anna Maria*, and the *Empress of England* was sold to the Shaw Savill Line in 1970 to become the *Ocean Monarch*. Refitted for her new role by Cammell Laird at Birkenhead, the *Ocean Monarch* was not ready for her scheduled inaugural voyage to New Zealand in March and finally sailed in October. When she did sail she carried 70 waitresses – no fewer than 1,200 girls had applied for the jobs! Cammell Laird declared a loss on the £2 million job, which they attributed to a serious miscalculation of the amount of work involved. Notwithstanding, the ship looked outwardly similar before and after the refit. Used mainly for cruising as a one-class ship with accommodation for 1,200 passengers, she was eventually withdrawn in 1974 and scrapped. The *Empress of England* and *Empress of Canada* had adopted a garish two-tone green and white funnel in 1968.

The *Empress of Canada* was sold in 1972 for further service. She had closed the transatlantic service in November 1971, ending the company's 80 year association with passenger traffic on the North Atlantic and Pacific and ending Liverpool's long connection with the North Atlantic passenger trade. As she lay at Tilbury under her new owner's name of *Mardi Gras*, the National Seaman's Union began to picket the berth until her port of registration had been changed and the Red Ensign had been finally lowered in favour of the Panamanian flag. The *Mardi Gras* left Tilbury for Miami in February 1972. After a separation of 11 years, the *Mardi Gras* was joined by her former running-mate the *Empress of Britain*, when she left the Greek Line to join Carnivale Cruise Line as the *Carnivale* in 1976.

On the South American trades, cargo revenue was always a key factor to profitability. Labour disputes in the London docks in the early 1960s meant that many sailings returned part cargoes to their port of embarkation. To cap this, the beef import trade from South America collapsed, leaving a number of companies very exposed (see Chapter 4). The post-war flagship of the South American services was the Royal Mail Line's *Andes*. She was launched in March 1939 and her maiden voyage, which had been scheduled for September, was cancelled while the new ship was refitted as a troopship, with a capacity for over 4,000 men. Her maiden commercial voyage to the east coast of South America eventually started from Southampton in January 1948, when the ship was finally fitted out with spacious accommodation for 324 first and 204 cabin class passengers. She was converted to a full time cruise ship only 11 years later.

In those days liner company brochures were available for the asking from travel agents. For the most part, these were dull printed texts of sailing schedules and fares. Only one, the Royal Mail Line's schedule, included pull-out and full colour deck layouts – for the passenger accommodation of the mighty *Andes*.

Based at Liverpool, the Pacific Steam Navigation Company offered a South American west coast liner service via Panama. The elderly two funnel liner *Reina del Pacifico*, dating from 1931, was given a new running mate when the attractive looking *Reina del Mar* first arrived in the Mersey from her builders, Harland & Wolff of Belfast, in the spring of 1956. The *Reina del Pacifico* was decorated internally with a predominant Moorish and Spanish flavour. There was a single corridor running the length of the ship, which connected the first class Winter Garden bar with the ship's library; along the way were the trappings of the hacienda, including tile and plaster walls and a wooden beamed ceiling. The new *Reina del Mar* carried three classes: 207 first, 216 cabin and 343 tourist class and had cargo spaces both fore and aft of the main passenger accommodation. Ports covered by the two ships included La Rochelle, Santander, Coruna, Bermuda, Nassau, Havana, Kingston, La Guaira, Curacao, Cartagena, Cristobal, La Libertad, Callao, Arica, Antofagasta and Valparaiso, with calls also at Vigo and Plymouth on the return trip.

Sadly, the *Reina del Pacifico* stranded on a reef at

A tug nudges the *Reina del Mar* (1956) alongside the Princes Landing Stage at Liverpool, prior to departure for South America in October 1963.

Bermuda in 1957, then lost a voyage due to generator failure. When, three months later, she lost a propeller at Havana, the writing was on the wall and she competed her last voyage in April 1958. The new *Reina del Mar* survived on the route for only seven years, before being restyled as a cruise ship with one-class accommodation for 1,047 passengers (see Chapter 8). It was stated at the time that the full effects of air travel, combined with the communist revolution in Cuba in 1961, had so reduced the passenger and cargo potential that the service was no longer viable using such a large passenger unit.

The Ocean Terminal in Southampton fell into disuse. Tilbury Landing Stage became a moss covered eyesore, and the Princes Landing Stage at Liverpool became home only to the Mersey ferry and the Isle of Man boat. An era of travel, the steamship era, had finally ended, little over a hundred years after the Victorians had introduced this main line concept of travel. Sustained by a constant trade of emigration, increasingly supported by business and occasional holiday travellers, the passenger liner always maintained an element of glamour. There was often news of film stars and celebrities travelling on this ship or

that, of exotic 'boat trains' from Waterloo and an impression of luxury, that suppressed the knowledge that many of these ships had austere accommodation and dreary wood panelling in all but the first class quarters.

Personal memories of the main line transatlantic liners vary. For my part, getting totally lost and disorientated as a guest in the crew's quarters on the *Queen Mary* alongside at Southampton, competes with memory of liners moored two and three deep at Liverpool and Southampton during the National Seaman's Union strike of May and June 1966. The saddest sight was the *Carmania* and *Franconia* laid-up alongside each other by the Mayflower Park in Southampton, awaiting buyers. But the best time of all was watching the *Ocean Monarch* locking-out into the Mersey (see photograph on page 43) with her brand new Shaw Savill Line livery barely dry and an almost completely new crew, save for half a dozen key Canadian Pacific officers. As she slid into Langton Lock in time for the tide that sunny spring morning in 1970, the charge hand warned the shore crew in loud Scouse, "Watch out lads – we've a right bunch of flowers here!"

The Canadian Pacific Line

The Canadian Pacific Railway became a shipowner in 1889, when a passenger service between Hong Kong and Vancouver was inaugurated. The railway company later bought a fleet of cargo ships from Elder, Dempster & Company, so that they could extend services beyond their land-bound railheads, not only across the Pacific but also across the Atlantic. The Canadian Pacific Line began passenger operations between Canada and Liverpool in 1914. The much acclaimed and luxurious liner *Empress of Britain* was built in 1931, but this magnificent ship was lost to a bombing and torpedo attack early in World War Two. The Canadian Pacific Line also commissioned four intermediate class liners with Duchess names in 1928 and 1929; two of these survived the war, the *Duchess of Bedford* which was then renamed *Empress of France*, and the *Duchess of Richmond* which became the first post-war *Empress of Canada*. Both these ships were products of the John Brown shipyard.

The *Empress of Scotland*, formerly the *Empress of Japan* in the pre-war transpacific fleet, joined the Liverpool-based ships in 1950, following the withdrawal of the company from passenger services in the Pacific. The *Empress of Scotland* outclassed her fleet mates in speed and regularly called at Greenock within the routine schedule. She was also the winter long distance cruise ship based at New York. She went on to become the Hamburg America Line's *Hanseatic* until an engine room fire at New York caused her withdrawal and subsequent demolition.

The old *Empress of Canada* was gutted by fire while alongside at Liverpool in 1953. The *Empress of France* remained in service until 1957, only then being displaced by the new sisters *Empress of Britain* and *Empress of England*. As a temporary measure pending new building, the *De Grasse* was purchased from French owners and placed in service as the *Empress of Australia*, later to be displaced from the fleet in December 1957. For a brief period that year a four-ship service was operated, but the *Empress of Scotland* was also withdrawn, so that by 1958 the Transatlantic route was left in the charge of the two new Empresses.

The new *Empress of Britain* and the *Empress of England* could carry 148 first class and 896 tourist class passengers. They were followed in 1961 by the last of the Canadian Pacific liners, the *Empress of Canada*. She had identical turbine machinery to the earlier pair, but was slightly beamier and consequently a little bit slower. This ship was built with a dual role of cruise ship and liner and displaced the *Empress of Britain* from her role as winter cruise ship, a role which the *Empress of Britain* had earlier inherited from the old *Empress of Scotland*.

These ships each had stern anchors, as did the Cunard *Saxonia*-class. This was to enable them to anchor fore and aft in the narrow confines of the St Lawrence. The distinctive recessed anchors were very much a badge of the liners built for the Quebec and Montreal routes.

3. Other Mainline Services

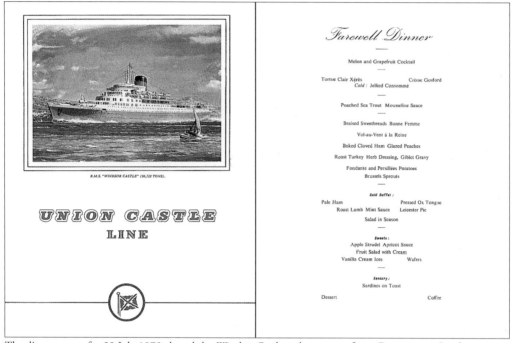

R.M.S. "WINDSOR CASTLE" (36,123 TONS).

UNION CASTLE
LINE

Farewell Dinner

Melon and Grapefruit Cocktail

Tortue Clair Xérès   Crème Gosford
Cold : Jellied Consommé

Poached Sea Trout Mousseline Sauce

Braised Sweetbreads Bonne Femme

Vol-au-Vent à la Reine

Baked Cloved Ham Glazed Peaches

Roast Turkey Herb Dressing, Giblet Gravy

Fondante and Persillées Potatoes
Brussels Sprouts

Cold Buffet :
Pale Ham   Pressed Ox Tongue
Roast Lamb Mint Sauce   Leicester Pie
Salad in Season

Sweets :
Apple Strudel Apricot Sauce
Fruit Salad with Cream
Vanilla Cream Ices   Wafers

Savoury :
Sardines on Toast

Dessert   Coffee

The dinner menu for 22 July 1973 aboard the *Windsor Castle* on her voyage from Capetown to Southampton.

The take-over by the jet airliner was somewhat slower on the African and Asian services than it had been over the North Atlantic, and it only began to affect the Far Eastern and Australian routes in the early 1970s. However, a number of other factors were also at work, and erosion of many of these routes started in the 1960s. One of the strangest downfalls was the Union Castle weekly mail-ship service between Southampton and Durban with intermediate stops in the Canaries, Capetown, Port Elizabeth and East London. This service was upgraded from a 14 day to an $11\frac{1}{2}$ day voyage to Capetown (see Chapter 1); but this required increased fuel consumption which, along with the onset of containerisation and a fleet of mail-ships only capable of handling break-bulk cargo, hastened the demise of the service.

The arrival of the *Windsor Castle* and *Transvaal Castle* on the service in 1960 and 1961 allowed the faster service to come into play. The elderly motorships *Athlone Castle* and *Stirling Castle* were withdrawn (they had in their day been instrumental in upgrading the mail-ship service to 14 days, but their diesel units were only capable of providing the service requirements with careful on board maintenance and not a little coaxing). The *Capetown Castle* was displaced to a secondary and slower support role by two fast freight only ships in 1965. These were the *Good Hope Castle* and the *Southampton Castle* and they worked alongside the 1948-built mail ships *Edinburgh Castle* and *Pretoria Castle* as well as the *Pendennis Castle*, broadly similar to the earlier pair but completed over a decade later in 1959. The *Pendennis Castle* made news on her maiden voyage as she was the

The *Stirling Castle* (1936) off the Royal Pier at Southampton at the start of another voyage to the Cape.

The *Pendennis Castle* (1958) leaving Southampton for the Cape in June 1968.

The *Edinburgh Castle* (1948) arriving at Capetown on passage from Durban to Southampton.

The *Pretoria Castle* (1948), as built with two masts, seen alongside at Southampton in August 1964.

first British passenger liner to carry waitresses (known as stewardettes) in the dining saloons. When the *Capetown Castle* was disposed of in 1967, the freight-only *Southampton Castle* and *Good Hope Castle* were fitted with accommodation for 12 passengers to service St Helena and Ascension. At that stage the mail ship service was, therefore, maintained by seven ships.

The weekly Friday departure from Southampton – traditionally at 1300 hours, but now displaced to 1600 hours – was maintained throughout the late 1960s and early 1970s. The company terminal moved from the Old Docks to new accommodation in 1956. From then on the inward ships came in to Berth 102, New Docks and moved along the quay to Berth 103 to prepare for departure. A modern passenger terminal was situated between the two.

The company was always proud of its mail-ships. Marischal Murray wrote in the company's centenary book, the *Union Castle Chronicle*, which was published in 1953:

> It was not by reason of speed and size that the *Stirling Castle* and *Athlone Castle* achieved distinction. Their passenger accommodation was outstanding and represented something entirely new, for in general layout these ships were quite unlike any of their predecessors. In the matter of cabins the usual amenities – though much improved – were, of course provided. As regards public rooms in the first class there was now the Long Gallery, a dignified apartment linking smoking room with lounge, while opening off the latter was a particularly charming drawing room furnished with impeccable taste. Most revolutionary, however, was the institution of a new class of accommodation, termed cabin class.

The accommodation on the *Athlone Castle* and *Stirling Castle*, and their younger near sister, the *Capetown Castle* (the first mail-ship in the fleet to be given a South African name in response to numerous requests), was designed to be light and airy, cool and extremely comfortable, without

being too lavish. Much use was made of indirect lighting aboard these ships. In pre-war days their cabin class was as good as first class in many ships. Being oil engined, and their machinery less than ideal for the express service, a reversion to steam turbine machinery was made for the post-war sisters *Edinburgh Castle* and *Pretoria Castle*.

The youngest passenger ship in the fleet, the *Transvaal Castle* and her 'Hotel Class' accommodation, was distinguished by having a bulbous bow. At her handing over ceremony, the managing director of the builders, John Brown of Clydebank, was appalled to discover that the name of the Union Castle Line chairman, Sir Nicholas Cayzer, had been misspelled with a 'K'. A replacement certificate had to be hastily drawn up!

Accelerating fuel oil costs in the early 1970s, together with the faster operational speeds and seasonal decline in passenger numbers, placed the economics of the service in jeopardy, even though the overall passenger demand remained reasonably buoyant. The mail-liner voyages to Capetown and the east coast of South Africa continued until 1977 when they were closed by the two remaining passenger ships, the *Windsor Castle* and *S A Vaal*, formerly the *Transvaal Castle*. Transfer of the latter ship and the *Pretoria Castle* (which had become the *S A Oranje*) to the South African Marine Corporation in 1966 resulted in their transfer to South African registry some three years later.

The only professional entertainers carried on the mail-ships were a pair of musicians. It was down to the officers to form cabaret teams, the casts for pantomime, variety, panel games and the obligatory 'Crossing the Line' ceremony. Bingo, race meetings and gambling on the day's run were routine passenger pastimes.

The *S A Oranje* completed her last voyage on 8 September 1975 and after destoring, sailed to Taiwan for demolition; the *Edinburgh Castle* was withdrawn the following April. The *Pendennis Castle* was also withdrawn in 1976 and after protracted lay up in Hong Kong harbour under various names, was demolished in 1980. The *S A Vaal* went on to serve as the cruise ship *Festivale*.

The *S A Vaal* (1961) shortly after transfer from the Union Castle Line in January 1969.

The *Windsor Castle* docked at Southampton for the last time in September 1977, later becoming a hotel ship at Jeddah, replacing the former Elder Dempster liner *Aureol* (Chapter 5) which then returned to Greece. Thereafter, the South African service was continued using container ships with no passenger facilities, although Safmarine twice attempted to run a passenger service, but with little success on either occasion. A number of other short lived attempts to renew the passenger link have been made over the years. None have survived long, other than Curnow Shipping who now maintain the link via St Helena, although with relatively limited passenger accommodation (Chapter 5).

Among the scandals, murders, and man-overboard incidents, the story of the missing gold bullion aboard the *Capetown Castle* on arrival at Southampton from Capetown, in February 1965, is one of the more bizarre. Gold bullion was normally unloaded even as the passengers disembarked, and was immediately taken on to

London by special train. However, on this occasion 20 gold bars, worth about £200,000, went missing between the ship's strong room and the quayside. Upon this discovery, no further personnel were allowed to leave before the ship was searched by police. Conspicuous splashing noises drew the Chief Officer's attention to a sufficient extent for him to order the lowering of a boat, only to discover some of the crew hastily abandoning certain illegal items (although not gold bars) through a porthole! All the stock rooms were laboriously searched, and eventually and reluctantly Southampton police released the ship and her passengers. The *Capetown Castle* sailed on time the following week. Two voyages later, police enquiries led to a pair of officers flying to Durban, where they found the missing bullion set in concrete in a sand box at the foot of the forward mast. Arrests were duly made and the appropriate crew members flown back to Britain to face trial.

On the Africa and Far East routes a significant influence on declining passenger numbers was the

S.A. ORANJE

LENGTH OVERALL: 740 FEET
BREADTH (MOULDED): 84 FEET
TONNAGE: 27,518 GROSS TONS

FIRST CLASS

1. Charthouse and Wheelhouse
2. Commander's Day Room
3. Officers' Accommodation
4. Radio Room

5. First Class Lounge
6. Cocktail Lounge
7. Long Gallery
8. First Class Smoke Room

9. First Class Verandah Café
10. Tourist Class Lounge
11. Tourist Class Verandah
12. Tourist Class Swimming Pool

13. Tourist Class Smoke Room
14. Tourist Class Childrens' Playroom
15. Tourist Class Recreation Space

16. First Class Cabins
17. De Luxe Cabins
18. First Class Shops
19. First Class Childrens' Playroom
20. Aft End of Crew's Accommodation
22. First Class Entrance and Bureau
23. Tourist Class Cabins
24. Tourist Class Entrance Hall, Shop and Bureau
25. Tourist Class Dining Saloon
26. First Class Dining Saloon
27. First Class Swimming Pool and Gymnasium

TOURIST CLASS

KEY TO SECTIONAL-ELEVATION

1. Charthouse and Wheelhouse
2. Commander's Day Room
3. Officers' Accommodation
4. Radio Room
5. First Class Lounge
6. Cocktail Lounge
7. Long Gallery
8. First Class Smoke Room
9. First Class Verandah Café

10. Tourist Class Lounge
11. Tourist Class Verandah Café
12. Tourist Class Swimming Pool
13. Tourist Class Smoke Room
14. Tourist Class Childrens' Playroom

15. Tourist Class Recreation Space
16. First Class Cabins
17. De Luxe Cabins
18. First Class Shop

19. First Class Childrens' Playroom
20. Aft End of Crew's Accommodation
22. First Class Entrance and Bureau
23. Tourist Class Cabins

24. Tourist Class Entrance Hall, Shop and Bureau
25. Tourist Class Dining Saloon
26. First Class Dining Saloon
27. First Class Swimming Pool and Gymnasium

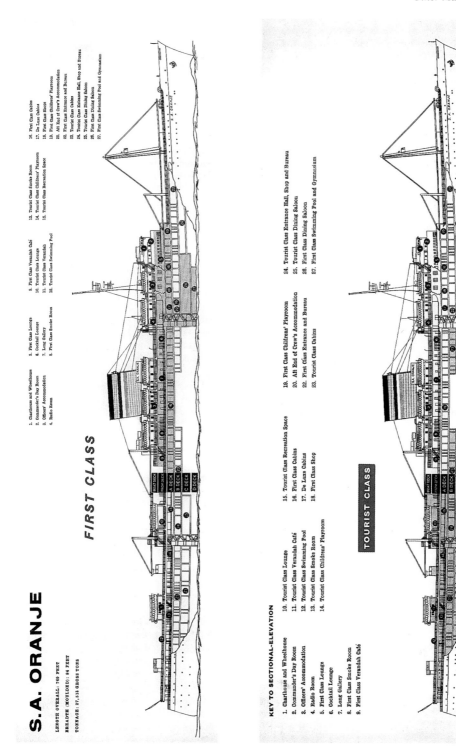

The *Canberra* (1961) at Southampton.

progressive independence of former colonial states. This greatly reduced the passenger demand, as colonial civil servants were replaced by a diminishing exchange of teachers, advisors and technical specialists who, in any case, took to the aeroplane. The services affected included those of British India, Union Castle (East African services), Elder Dempster and Anchor Line.

Throughout this decline the Australia run remained almost unaffected. P&O-Orient introduced new tonnage in the form of the *Oriana*, built in 1960 at a cost of £15 million, and the *Canberra* the following year. The pair effectively displaced the four pre-war Straths which were successively withdrawn by 1964. The combined P&O-Orient service otherwise continued much as it always had done, with regular departures via Suez to the Antipodes. It is interesting to note that the *Canberra*, for all her innovation, cost £16 million to build in 1961, whereas the *Himalaya* and the *Orcades* cost only £3 million in the immediate post-war years,

although three years later the cost of the *Oronsay* had risen to £4 million.

Innovation included the placing of the engines aft in *Canberra* and the use of all welded aluminium superstructure aboard *Oriana*. Mr Brian O'Rorke was the consultant in charge for the completion of the *Oriana*, just as 22 years before he had designed the much acclaimed interiors for the *Orion*. The ships adopted the court cabin system, whereby up to six cabins each had a narrow window into a small court, which in turn had porthole access to natural light. Most ships previously adopted the Bibby system, in which 'L' shaped cabins were stacked behind each other away from the hull, each with a narrow passageway leading to a porthole.

In post-war years, both P&O and Orient Line had built a series of unimaginative passenger and cargo liners to replace war losses and ageing tonnage. P&O put the quasi-sisters *Himalaya* and *Chusan* onto the Australian and Far Eastern services and followed them a few years later with

Launch of the *Orion* (1935), on 7 December 1934, into the Walney Channel at Barrow.   *The Sankey Collection*

The start of another liner voyage for the *Himalaya* (1949), Southampton, in February 1970.

The *Iberia* (1954) leaving Southampton in June 1969.

The *Orsova* (1954) arriving in the early morning at Southampton in May 1968.

The *Oronsay* (1951) passing the Royal Pier at Southampton at the start of a liner voyage in May 1969.

another pair, the *Iberia* and *Arcadia*, which went straight onto the round-the-world service. The *Arcadia* had stabilisers and partial air conditioning when built; full air conditioning was installed in 1961. Meanwhile, the Orient Line brought out the *Orcades* and *Oronsay*, and later a third and broadly similar ship, the *Orsova*, which was launched the same day as the *Arcadia* in May 1953. All three were deployed on the round-the-world service which was based out of London. The deployment of these new ships reduced the passage time to Melbourne by ten days to only 28 days.

In the days when many of the passengers were families travelling to a new life as assisted passage migrants, on-board school was organised for the under 12s. The emphasis was not so much on education but rather on giving the parents some respite during the day. At the start of the voyage all the teachers identified from the passenger list were co-opted to the scheme. The leading role was carried by the children's hostess, usually an energetic young woman who liked painting, making fancy dress costumes, Christmas decorations and the like, and encouraging music making around a piano. The term 'hostess' bears little resemblance to the 'entertainment hostess' of contemporary cruise ships, in which the role has developed more into the entertainment officer and cruise director. Entertainment only became a feature on the liners when competition between companies evolved, as the aeroplane began to cream away some of the previously plentiful patronage. As a consequence, by 1990, the *Oriana* was carrying around 60 entertainers on cruise trips.

The ship's doctor was usually kept busy particularly at the start of a voyage and, strangely, at the end. In the days before air conditioning, passengers were offered camp beds to sleep on deck in the tropics, although they had to be up early before the deck crew arrived to wash down the decks. At the end of one Orient Line voyage the doctor's story goes like this:

> I would like something for my wife, said the man awkwardly, kissing his wife goodbye and leaving the surgery as if he would never see her again.
>
> What is the trouble?
>
> My stomach is so upset.
>
> How long have you been unwell?
>
> Ever since we came on board at Tilbury, we're getting off tomorrow and I don't want to be ill when we land.
>
> Do you mean that you have been ill all the way from England?
>
> That's right, I wasn't well when I got on board but I thought you only treated seasick cases on the ship. My husband tried to get something for it at the places we stopped, but none of the medicines did any good. I have had an awful trip and he said I shouldn't flush the lavatory when the ship was stopped in harbour!

A remedy was produced that would have solved the problem weeks earlier, had it been requested.

The ships of the Orient Line always looked attractive with their 'corn'-coloured hulls and distinctive cowl-topped funnels, although they adopted the all white hull of P&O in 1964, some years after the two companies merged. Up and until then the sailings were fully co-ordinated and a seemingly integrated service to the Far East and Australia was offered, albeit by two separate shipping companies.

The ships received only minor modification during their careers. P&O's *Himalaya*, for example, changed slightly in appearance when she was given a smoke deflector funnel top in 1951. Otherwise the *Himalaya* received full air conditioning and was fitted with stabilisers between 1959 and 1961, and in 1963 was converted to one class. Other changes included the installation of a cinema over the engine casing on the Promenade Deck. Her main dining rooms were restyled the Drake Restaurant (formerly the first class dining saloon on D Deck) and the Tasman Restaurant (the former tourist class dining saloon). The Drake Restaurant, which extended the full width of the ship, and the former first class lounge on the Promenade Deck were furnished in panelling, engraved mirrors and drapes.

The pre-war liners continued to be disposed of in 1962, when the Australian government decided not to take up large numbers of berths

The Orient Line's *Orontes* (1929) never wore the company's distinctive corn coloured hull. *Author's Collection*

provisionally reserved for British migrants during the first half of the year. The withdrawal of the P&O *Strathnaver*, and the Orient liner *Orontes*, which had retained her black hull to the end, was brought forward and both ships were sold for scrap. They had ended their days on the Tilbury to Australia route converted to one-class ships, carrying 1,250 and 1,370 passengers respectively. The *Strathaird* had gone to the breaker's yard only the year before and at the same time the *Canton*, built in 1938 by Alexander Stephen on the Clyde, was withdrawn from the Tilbury Far East service.

Following war service the *Canton* had served well to become a firm favourite with travellers – she could accommodate 300 first and 244 tourist class passengers. These were the days when a wind chute was kept under the sink by the porthole for use in the tropics. (The chute was a semi-cone-shaped device that could be attached to the outside of the porthole so that it drew air into the cabin to create a cooling draught towards the open cabin door.) Film shows were held on deck with the screen attached to the main mast, projecting 35 mm film from a small steel hut on the Boat Deck. With assisted migrant passages outward, tourist class was relatively spacious on the return leg. However, many of the passengers were nurses and office workers returning on leave and the ship's officers had to keep an eye on their crew, given a determination to enjoy the voyage with such an imbalance of young women to men.

Next of the pre-war ships to be withdrawn was the *Orion*, which had been occupied on the Tilbury to Australia route, other than during the war, since she was completed in 1935. The last of the Straths, the *Strathmore* dating from 1935 and the *Strathaird* from 1937, were withdrawn in 1964. These ships had turbine machinery and single funnels. Their earlier sisters were completed with three funnels and had turbo-electric machinery pioneered by the famous *Viceroy of India*. Before going together to Greek ownership and further service, the *Stratheden* did a series of four cruises for the newly formed Travel Savings Association (see Chapter 8).

The last ships ordered for the liner service by the Orient Line and P&O were both something quite different and of completely new design. They were ordered on the strength of the transpacific passenger requirements, whereby large ships with a high passenger capacity could be operated cost effectively. The Orient Line commissioned the *Oriana* in December 1960, and her fast speed of 27 knots enabled her to reduce the crossing time between the UK and Sydney by one week to three weeks, thence on to San Francisco and Los Angeles and returning the same way. Her size, at 41,923 tons, required her to forsake London and operate from Southampton. She had accommodation for 638 first and 1,496 tourist class passengers and attractive and contemporary internal décor, which was widely acclaimed by both the UK and the Australian press.

Only six months later the new P&O flagship *Canberra* commenced her maiden voyage from Southampton, in June 1961. She too was bigger than the earlier succession of post war builds, with a tonnage of 45,733 and finely appointed accommodation for 556 first and 1,616 tourist class passengers. She was also capable of a three week passage time to Sydney. The *Canberra* had a striking outline, with innovative turbo-electric engines and funnels placed right aft, along the lines of the Shaw Savill liner *Southern Cross*. The two ships were an immediate success and quickly developed their own mark on the travelling public. However, the collision of the *Oriana* with the American aircraft carrier USS *Keasage* off Long Beach, California in December 1962, and fire aboard the *Canberra* the following month off the Italian coast, tarnished the image. In any case, success was to be short lived, as both ships were transferred to P&O Cruises in 1973 after only a dozen years in the liner trade. Both ships had operated occasional cruises between liner voyages.

In October 1966 the title P&O-Orient Lines, which had been adopted in 1960, was dropped in favour of P&O. In this way the 88 years service of the Orient Line suddenly disappeared once and for all.

Strangely the *Canberra* had been earmarked for disposal in February 1973 as being of too deep a draught (10.8 m) to enter many ports attractive to cruise customers. A feasibility study was carried out to see if re-engining the ship with diesels could alleviate the draught problem. A P&O press bulletin read: "The *Canberra* was built for the UK–Australia route and has the biggest passenger capacity of any liner afloat. But that route is no longer viable throughout the year, nor is the ship we built for it." Indeed she had lost £5 million in her New York cruise programme over the preceding two years. However, she was fully air conditioned and given suitable marketing was attractive in terms of economy of scale, with a passenger capacity of over 2,000. In the end, and given an improvement in the cruise market, the company wisely decided to sell the *Orsova* and retain the *Canberra*.

The *Canberra* became highly successful in her cruising role and survived until 1997. At that time she had developed a personal following and many passengers went back year after year to this same ship. Many commentators reported that towards the end of her career she had become a piece of history, with celebrated service in the Falklands War (Chapter 10), and by now extremely dated décor. She was almost the final passenger steam powered unit in the British merchant navy (the *Sky Princess* was the last – see Chapter 11), and there was an emotive pre-retiral encounter of the *Canberra* and the steam powered Royal Yacht *Britannia* when they last met in 1997.

The *Himalaya*, which had been designed for the UK–India–Sri Lanka–Australia service, also ran on the cross-Pacific service from west coast American and Canadian ports. This service had been inaugurated in 1954, when the Canadian-Australasian Line withdrew their ageing steamer *Aorangi* from the route. The *Himalaya* also ran a highly successful cruise programme in later years. She finally arrived in Taiwan for demolition in November 1975. Her consorts on the trans-Pacific service were the *Arcadia*, *Iberia*, *Chusan* and *Canberra*. The *Oronsay* was sold for demolition in 1975. The *Arcadia* was replaced by the former *Kungsholm* when she joined the P&O fleet as the *Sea Princess* (Chapter 10) in 1979. Like so many others, the *Arcadia* also ended up on the ship breaker's beach in Taiwan.

Shaw Savill also put new tonnage into the Australia/New Zealand passenger route, only in this case staking everything on passenger revenue. The Shaw Savill Line had originated in 1882 from

The *Southern Cross* (1955) turning to head down Southampton Water in June 1968.

the amalgamation of the fleets of Robert Shaw and Walker Saville with the Albion Line of Glasgow. In 1955 the company replaced two elderly cargo and passenger steamers on the Australian route with the innovative new-building *Southern Cross*. She was placed alongside the elderly flagship of the fleet, the *Dominion Monarch*. The *Southern Cross* was a striking ship which had been built by Harland & Wolff, with a capacity for 1,100 tourist class passengers but no cargo. It was said at the time that this was generally accepted as an answer to the strike-prone Australian docker, who was then making passenger and cargo ship schedules almost impossible to maintain.

The *Dominion Monarch* was also a remarkable ship, built, in 1939, for a new fast service to New Zealand via Capetown and Australia. In common with the Pacific Steam Navigation Company's *Reina del Pacifico* (Chapter 2), she had the almost unique combination of quadruple screws and four oil engines which gave her a service speed of 19 knots. She was a one-class ship with accommodation for 517 passengers, of which 129 had single berth cabins, each with its own telephone (ie there were no electric bells!). There

was a children's playroom, a swimming 'bath', gymnasium, veranda and 'Palm Court'-style lounge. The round voyage took just three and a half months. The war had intervened before a sister could be considered and in post-war years the need was more for a passenger-only ship to carry over 1,000, without being encumbered by cargo loading problems at either end of the voyage.

Consequently, the new *Southern Cross* was a complete contrast. The idea for the ship came from Basil Sanderson, long time manager of the Shaw Savill Line. The *Southern Cross* had traditional steam turbine machinery but this was placed aft, leaving an uncluttered ship for public room spaces and open decks. The placement of the machinery allowed an additional 20 cabins to be fitted, but the beam of the ship was slightly wider than a conventional ship of her size. Unhappily, the Ministry of Transport were concerned about trim and insisted on 1,000 tons of additional ballast being placed amidships, which required considerable redesign while she was under construction. Notwithstanding, the new ship quickly settled down into the round-the-

The imposing and majestic *Dominion Monarch* (1939) seen from the air in the English Channel.   *Foto Flite*

world service alternating east-about and west-about via Bermuda, Trinidad, Curacao, Panama, Tahiti, Fiji, Wellington, Aukland, Sydney, Melbourne, Freemantle, Durban, Capetown, Las Palmas and back to Southampton. In her first year she also undertook three short Mediterranean cruises. The scheduled liner voyage time was 76 days and she made four round trips per year.

Following the retirement of the *Dominion Monarch* in 1961, the *Southern Cross* was joined in 1962 by a quasi sister, the *Northern Star*. This ship had a greater passenger complement of 1,437, again tourist class only. The main differences were an observation deck at bridge level and two working alleyways, instead of the unconventional single alleyway on the *Southern Cross*. Neither was there an indoor swimming pool (a spectacularly unsuccessful feature aboard the *Southern Cross* in rough weather!) and the cabins which would otherwise have been under the 'Tavern', with its nocturnal noises, were resited. The two ships were marketed as 'The Splendid Sisters'.

On departure from Southampton it was customary to anchor off Cowes 'for full scale drills for passengers and crew lasting about one hour'. There were strict rules about children, who had their own special deck areas, rooms and swimming pools, as well as dedicated staff to cater and care for them. Children were not, however, allowed into the 'Tavern' at any time and their only access to the sports deck was during their own competitions.

The rising costs of maintaining the ships so that they conformed with changing regulations, plus increasing operating costs, saw the withdrawal of the *Southern Cross* in 1971. She ended service under the Red Ensign with four cruises from Liverpool and a final round-the-world voyage. Following considerable renovation and upgrading, she later returned to the UK cruise market under charter to Thomson cruises as the Greek ship *Calypso*, only being broken up in 1981 under the further name of *Azure Sea*.

From 1971 the *Northern Star* was increasingly used for cruising. By the autumn of 1975, hiked fuel costs put an end to the cruises and she was

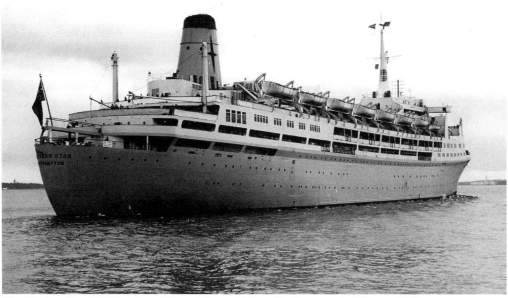

The *Northern Star* (1962) setting off around the world from Southampton in February 1969.

The *Ocean Monarch* (1957) gingerly setting off from Langton Dock, Liverpool, on her inaugural voyage for the Shaw Savill Line on 11 April 1970.

scrapped at the tender age of only thirteen. The *Northern Star* had in any case begun to suffer serious mechanical difficulties, when boiler tube failure terminated a Mediterranean cruise only the year before. In 1974, the *Ocean Monarch*, which joined the fleet from Canadian Pacific in 1970 (Chapter 2), also suffered severe mechanical difficulties and was withdrawn from service in June 1975 and sold for demolition. Passengers booked on the scheduled summer cruises and later liner voyages of the *Ocean Monarch* were found berths on the *Northern Star*.

Time finally caught up in the early 1970s, a good ten years after the transatlantic services had been decimated. Significantly, the Jumbo jet now began to serve beyond the Middle East, and the container ship also commenced service between Europe, the Far East and Australasia. The final regular liner voyages to Australia took place in 1973, after which P&O liner expertise was concentrated on the newly formed P&O Cruises, initially with only three ships. The *Arcadia* left the fleet in 1979, and P&O Cruises sustained the *Oriana* from 1973 until her withdrawal in 1986, while the *Canberra* was able to continue cruising until 1997.

Other liners which had managed to remain in service only after conversion to cruise ships, were also progressively taken out of service throughout the 1970s. Some went prematurely to the breaker's yard, others were sold on for service with new owners under foreign flags, and some were even used as accommodation ships. Not one of the main line routes survived, and only one liner remains in service under the Red Ensign now that the airliner has established its supremacy, as the passenger numbers for the port of Southampton reflect only too well (Figure 2 overleaf).

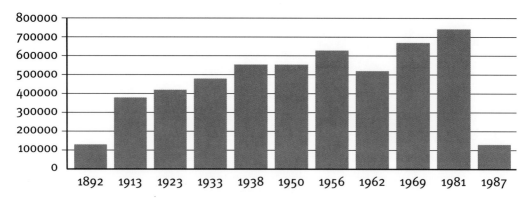

Figure 2: Southampton ocean liner passenger numbers for selected years

The Post-War Emigrant Ships

To Australia

From 1947	*Ormonde* built 1918 (Orient Line)
From 1948	*Ranchi* built 1925 (P&O)
	Chitral built 1925 (P&O)
	Somersetshire built 1921 (Bibby Line)
	Dorsetshire built 1920 (Bibby Line)
	Amarapoora built 1920 (Henderson Line)
From 1949	*Georgic* built 1931 (Cunard White Star Line)
	Asturias built 1926 (Royal Mail Line)
	Oxfordshire built 1912 (Bibby Line)
	Cheshire built 1927 (Bibby Line)
	Empire Clyde, ex-*Cameronia* built 1921 (Anchor Line)
	New Australia, ex-*Monarch of Bermuda* built 1931 (Shaw Savill & Albion), became Greek Line *Arkadia* in 1958.

To New Zealand

From 1948	*Atlantis*, ex-*Andes* built 1913 (Royal Mail Line)
From 1952	*Captain Cook*, ex-*Letitia*, ex-*Empire Brent* built 1924 (Donaldson Line)
	Captain Hobson built 1920 ex-*Amarapoora* (Henderson Line)

By 1955 only the *Georgic*, *New Australia*, *Captain Cook* and *Captain Hobson* remained in service. The *Captain Cook* made seven transatlantic voyages on the Donaldson Line service as a diversion from the emigrant trade during 1955. Subsequently, of the emigrant ships remaining in service, the *Georgic* was withdrawn in 1956, the *New Australia* in 1957, the *Captain Hobson* in 1958 and the *Captain Cook* in February 1960, so ending the Ministry of Transport service. Thereafter, the emigrants were accommodated by the British liner services or occasional charters.

4. Lesser Routes – The Americas

A diverse range of other passenger services was available from UK ports in the 1950s and 1960s. Although many of these could also be described as main line services, they were distinguished by their dual dependence on passenger and cargo revenue. Service speeds tended to be a little more leisurely and schedules were subject to change, depending on cargo handling requirements. The ships themselves almost always offered first class accommodation, but none compared with that offered by the prestigious liners on the North Atlantic.

Many of the lesser routes had their own distinctive flavours. The Royal Mail Line ships on South American routes were as much at home to Spanish as they were to English speaking travellers, much as the Asian seamen aboard ships of British India, P&O and others gave them a unique oriental character. The Fyffe Line banana boats were a complete contrast, offering first class only accommodation to round trippers. But it was never quite clear whether the vermin traps on the mooring lines were to keep the ship's rats from gaining the shore, or to prevent the dockside rats from emigrating!

On the Western Ocean there were a number of passenger cargo liners operating well into the 1960s. Liverpool was host to the Furness Warren Line service to St John's, Newfoundland and Halifax, Nova Scotia, terminating at Boston. The service was maintained by the *Nova Scotia* and *Newfoundland* which had been built by Vickers Armstrong in 1947 and 1948 respectively. Their hulls were strengthened for operation in ice. They had comfortable accommodation for 62 first class and 96 tourist class passengers and attracted a regular travelling clientele, especially in the summer season. One reason given for lack of

The *Newfoundland* (1947) entering the Mersey from Langton Lock.   *J & M Clarkson Collection*

The *Media* (1948) at the Princes Landing Stage, Liverpool, collecting passengers for New York in July 1959.

patronage in the winter months was the small size of the ships in rough conditions; both ships were reduced to carry only 12 passengers in 1962 and were sold for further service the following year.

The only Scottish service to Canada was reinstated by the Donaldson Line after the war, partly at the request of the Scottish Tourist Board. Donaldson had purchased two American 'Victory'-type ships in 1946: the *Laurentia*, built as the *Medina Victory*, and the *Lismoria*, formerly the *Taos Victory*. Accommodation was installed on the ships for 55 one class passengers, and the service from Glasgow to Montreal was inaugurated in October 1948 by the *Lismoria*. At a reception on board, the Scottish Tourist Board stated it would do its utmost to see that the enterprise of the Donaldson Line met with its merited response.

For the following 18 years the *Lismoria* and *Laurentia* maintained the St Lawrence season (April to November) from Glasgow to Quebec and Montreal, and in the winter ran between Liverpool through the Panama Canal to Los Angeles, San Francisco and Vancouver. At the end of the 1966 season the passenger service was withdrawn on the grounds of heavy service costs. The ageing pair of ships were sold shortly afterwards for demolition.

Cunard converted two Brocklebank cargo ships on the stocks into intermediate passenger and cargo liners for the Liverpool to New York service. These were the *Media* and *Parthia* which were delivered, in 1947 and 1948 respectively, by John Brown on the Clyde and Harland & Wolff at Belfast. The *Media* was the first post-war new build passenger ship for the North Atlantic. The ships could accommodate 250 one class passengers, while the public rooms comprised cinema/lounge, long gallery, drawing and writing room, entrance hall and a smoking room on the Promenade Deck, with the dining room on the Main Deck. In 1961 the *Media* was sold for further service as the *Flavia* and based at Genoa. The *Parthia* went on to become the New Zealand Line's *Remuera* (Chapter 5).

The banana boats of Elders & Fyffes Limited (a wholly owned, but British flagged, subsidiary of the American owned United Fruit Company) had

The *Golfito* (1949) leaving Empress Dock at Southampton in October 1968 in the original funnel colours.

always carried passengers on its services to the Caribbean. Post-war build, the *Golfito* (named after a banana port in Costa Rica) brought a new standard to the service, with first class accommodation for 111 passengers. She was not a big ship, with a gross tonnage of only 8,740, but was a graceful looking steamer, with a silver grey hull and plain yellow and black topped funnel. It was hoped that the pre-war round trip with three days in a popular hotel would soon pick up again. At first she was based at Rotterdam, but transferred to Southampton in 1952 (the cargo-only ships still ran to Avonmouth or Garston until 1967). She had actually been built with an eye to the New York trade of her parent group the United Fruit Company, but she never actually sailed on that service.

Running mates for the *Golfito* were the elderly but rather graceful looking *Ariguani*, *Bayano* and *Cavina*. These were replaced in November 1956 when the new steamer *Camito* arrived at Southampton from her builders, Alexander Stephen & Sons, on the Clyde. The new ship had a capacity for 103 first class passengers and ten

children in single and double berth cabins, arranged on the Bridge and Promenade Decks. There were also two suites at the forward end of the Bridge Deck, each comprising a day room, bedroom and bathroom. The lounge, ballroom and swimming pool were all on the Promenade Deck and the smoking room, bar, library and writing room were situated on either side of the engine room casing on this same deck. The entrance hall, purser's office, the shop and hairdressing saloon were on the Bridge Deck and the dining saloon was on the Upper Deck.

The ship was notable for the complete system of fire protection afforded by internal construction with proofed materials. Both the *Camito* and *Golfito* had large lounges with a dance floor, cinema, swimming pool and other extras previously unseen on the route. They were both fitted with air conditioning at the end of the 1966 season, and both adopted the attractive funnel colours of their parent company during the 1969–70 winter refits. As turbine steamers they found the escalating running costs of the early 1970s too much to cope with and were

Elders & Fyffes' *Camito* (1956) seen in United Fruit Company colours at Southampton in May 1970.

withdrawn successively in 1971 and 1972.

No longer was it possible to spend a month cruising across the Atlantic and back on a Fyffes banana boat. However, Geest Industries Limited banana boats running to Barry were equipped with limited passenger accommodation. For example, the *Geesttide*, completed in 1971 could carry ten passengers in three double and four single cabins, and had a distinctive lounge and bar across the full width of the Bridge Deck, the sole preserve of the passengers. Geest discontinued passenger carrying in 1995 with the sale of the *Geestport* and *Geestbay*.

Advertised for many years by the slogan '1,000 miles up the Amazon by Booth Liner', the Liverpool-based service terminating at Manaus was always popular, particularly as a round trip. The last two passenger ships on the run were the *Hubert* and the *Anselm*, the latter bought from Cie Maritime Belge in 1961. She was formerly the *Thysville*, and previous to that the *Baudouinville*, built in 1950 as one of five identical sisters. She

was released from her service to the Congo when that state became independent and the life style of the expatriate population became untenable. The *Hubert* was completed in 1955, with accommodation for 74 first class and 96 tourist class passengers. She was a near sister to the *Hildebrand* which entered service in 1951. The third passenger ship on the route was the *Hilary* which dated from 1931; she was converted from coal burning in 1949 and received a major refit in 1955 to bring her into line with the new ships. Their route took them to Leixoes, Lisbon, Madeira and Belem, and thence to the Amazon. After 1956 the route was extended to include Barbados and Trinidad. The *Hildebrand* was lost in 1957 when she was wrecked off the Portugese coast, after she went ashore off Cascais, and had to be abandoned a month later. The elderly *Hilary* was withdrawn and scrapped in 1959. This left the *Hubert* to maintain the passenger-cargo service which complemented a cargo only service from New York to the Amazon. The passenger

The *Hubert* (1955) in the Brocklebank Branch Dock, Liverpool, opposite the *Scottish Star* (1950) in July 1964. The *Scottish Star* was one of a number of British cargo liners to be trapped in the Great Bitter Lake in the Suez Canal between 1967 and 1975.

ships also undertook occasional cruises.

The *Anselm* had a capacity of 10, 950 gross tons and accommodation for 128 first class and 101 tourist class passengers; she was far and away the largest merchant ship to sail up the Amazon. However, passenger traffic began to fail soon after she entered service with the Booth Line. After only two years she was transferred within the Vestey Group to the Blue Star Line, and with reduced passenger capacity of 76 first class only, she became the *Iberia Star* on the London to the River Plate service (see below). The *Hubert* returned to Liverpool from her last voyage on 1 October 1964. She was promptly sold for use out of Singapore by the Austasia Line as the *Malaysia*; later sold to Middle East interests, and eventually scrapped in 1984.

The Royal Mail Line maintained a prestigious service between London and Buenos Aires, with intermediate calls at Cherbourg (outward), Boulogne (return), Vigo, Lisbon, Las Palmas, Rio de Janeiro, Santos and Montevideo. There was always a strong romantic attachment to the Royal Mail Line which was summed up by Rudyard Kipling's well known lines:

"Yes, weekly from Southampton,
Great steamers, white and gold,
Go rolling down to Rio
(Roll down – roll down to Rio!)
And I'd like to roll to Rio
Some day before I'm old!"

In the post-war years the Royal Mail Line passenger service was maintained by the *Highland Brigade, Highland Princess, Highland Chieftain* and the *Highland Monarch*. They had been completed between 1928 and 1930 for the former Nelson Line, which had been acquired by the Royal Mail Line before the Great War.

The fifth ship was the *Highland Hope,* which only survived until 1930 when she was wrecked outward bound from Vigo to Lisbon. Her

(Continued on page 52)

The *Arlanza* (1960) coming into Southampton during June 1968.

Looking the worse for wear, the *Aragon* (1960) is seen leaving Southampton in February 1969.

The *Argentina Star* (1947) at Southampton – note the different funnel-top arrangements on the four sisters.

The *Brazil Star* (1947) leaving Southampton in October 1968.

(Continued from page 49)
replacement, the *Highland Patriot*, completed in 1932, was sunk by torpedo in October 1940. A further replacement, this time without a Highland name, was laid down in 1946 and completed in 1948. She was the *Magdelena* of 17,547 tons gross, with a capacity for 133 first class and 346 third class passengers. She was equipped with steam turbine engines and had a service speed of 18 knots; this greater speed over the *Highland*-class motor ships allowed additional ports of call within the schedule. She was a most attractive looking ship with a large central funnel. Her profile mirrored that of the *Highland*-class and her successors the *Amazon*, *Aragon* and *Arlanza*, with a distinctive isolated 'island' bridge structure forward of the deeply trunked No 3 hatch. She was the first British liner to have air conditioning throughout her first class accommodation.

On the afternoon of 24 April 1949 she sailed from Santos bound for Rio de Janeiro. The voyage required a reduced speed of 13 knots to achieve a daylight arrival. Visibility was good. She had the best navigational aids of the day, radar, even double watches on the bridge, yet she strayed so far off course that at 0440 hours the next morning she hit a well charted reef, just 25 km out of Rio.

Although she was refloated, she was low in the water with severe bottom damage, and she broke her back when being towed in heavy swell over the bar outside Rio. The neglect of the master was stated to be "a grave dereliction of duty".

Three very attractive looking sisters were built by Harland & Wolff of Belfast to replace the surviving ships of the *Highland*-class, for the service in 1959 and 1960. These were the *Amazon*, *Arlanza* and *Aragon*. Like other ships in the South American trade, they had large refrigerated cargo capacity, but also passenger accommodation for 92 first class and 82 cabin class, although some cabins were used in either class depending on demand, as well as 275 third class. Their arrival in service displaced the elderly former Nelson Line vessels, and allowed the *Andes* (see Chapter 2) to become a full time cruise ship.

All went well with the new ships, which were dubbed 'The Three Graces', until there was a ban on meat imports from the River Plate to the UK in early 1968. This had the immediate effect of displacing the *Amazon* from the service. She was sold to the Shaw Savill Line to become the *Akaroa* (see Chapter 5). The *Arlanza* completed her last round trip between 7 December 1968 and 24 January 1969, followed by the *Aragon* sailing from

The *Paraguay Star* (1948) passing down the Thames off Gravesend in December 1966.

The *Uruguay Star* (1948) setting out from Southampton in March 1968.

London on 4 January 1969 and returning on 21 February, thereby closing an important era of passenger transport. Both ships then joined their sister on the Shaw Savill round-the-world service.

Before the *Iberia Star* joined Blue Star Line, four sisters, the *Argentina Star*, *Brasil Star*, *Uruguay Star* and *Paraguay Star* had maintained the South American service. These ships were built by Cammell Laird at Birkenhead between 1947 and 1948. Departures from London every two to three weeks were to Lisbon, Madeira, Las Palmas, Tenerife, Recife, Salvador, Rio de Janeiro, Santos and Montevideo, terminating at Buenos Aires. The ships carried a crew of 91 and had well appointed accommodation for 53 first class passengers (51 in the *Argentina Star*) in spacious cabins or staterooms on the Bridge Deck and Passenger Deck. Almost all the cabins had private bathrooms. There was a lounge, smoke room, verandah and dining saloon which had very large windows to give maximum light. There was also a children's room, shop and hairdressing salon.

A sunken swimming pool was situated at the fore end of the Bridge Deck (beneath the Sun Deck) which was protected by a glazed screen. They became very popular with the travelling public, in addition to providing a fast (16 knot) cargo liner service, returning with chilled and frozen Argentinian beef.

The service continued until 1969 when the *Paraguay Star* suffered serious damage by fire while unloading in the Royal Victoria Dock in London. The incident occurred during inspection of her steam turbine machinery, with fire breaking out in the engine room when a generator ignited an oil tank. With 25 fire appliances and a fire float, the fire was eventually brought under control, but the ship was beyond economic repair and was later broken up. The three surviving sisters were also withdrawn in 1972. They had served their owners well, but finally became victims of containerisation.

5. Lesser Routes – Africa, Asia and Australia

The 'White Swan', the *Aureol* (1951), entering the Mersey from the Langton Lock in September 1966.

The fortnightly mail-ship service between Liverpool, Lagos and Apapa, calling at Las Palmas, Freetown and Takoradi was provided by the Elder Dempster Line flagship *Aureol* and her two fleet mates the *Accra* and *Apapa*. Standards were extremely high on the mail-ships with extensive menus, high tea with cucumber sandwiches and French pastries, and in addition ice cream was usually available on deck while the ships were in the tropics. Passenger entertainment included bridge schools, bingo, deck tennis, quoits, horse racing (with dice and pulleys) and cricket (using a soft ball). Serving, as they did, the British community in West Africa, these ships employed an increasing complement of West African deck officers, many of whom had learnt their trade in the company training ship *Sulima* in the early 1960s. This ship had been

converted for this role in 1959, having been built for the company with limited passenger accommodation in 1948.

The *Aureol* was perhaps the most attractive of all the post-war liners. Built by Alexander Stephen & Sons at Glasgow in 1951, she had twin Doxford diesels which gave her a service speed of 16 knots. She could accommodate 253 first and 100 cabin class passengers, but also had space for 3,000 tons of cargo. There was a swimming pool, a shop and a hairdresser's. Part air conditioning was installed and this was upgraded in 1960 to include all the cabins and public rooms.

The rather more functional looking *Accra* and *Apapa* offered similar first class accommodation with 259 berths, with cots available for 30 children, plus accommodation for 24 third class passengers. They were both products of Vickers

The *Accra* (1947) seen in the River Mersey in July 1967.

The *Apapa* (1948) approaches Princes Landing Stage, Liverpool, dressed fore and aft ready to take the President of Nigeria back home after a state visit.

Armstrong at Barrow, the *Accra* in 1947 and the *Apapa* a year later. They received air conditioning in the first class cabins only in 1960, and survived until 1967 and 1968 respectively, the service suffering at that time from political instability in West Africa. The *Apapa* was reported to have completed 177 round voyages, steamed 1.6 million kilometres and carried over 100,000 passengers and 750,000 tons of cargo during her career. The *Aureol* continued alone on the service and carried out some cruises in 1967, but they were not a success. From 1972 the *Aureol* was based at Southampton, before she too was withdrawn, closing the West Africa service in 1974. She was sold for use as an accommodation ship at Jeddah and then laid up in Greece in 1989, only to be broken up 12 years later.

Two elderly steam ships joined the Elder Dempster fleet from the Natal Line in 1957.

These were the *Calabar* and *Winneba*, formerly the *Umtali* and *Umtata*, built in 1936 and 1938 respectively for their owner's UK to South Africa service. They lasted only six years under the Elder Dempster flag, where they inaugurated a new London to West Africa service before its withdrawal in 1963. They provided a departure from London every four weeks, and company publicity material stated: "Before they began their new role they were extensively refitted and improved. Each ship carries 105 passengers in one class and for their enjoyment has a library, a lounge, a swimming pool and a particularly spacious sports deck." Advertised as the 'Express Service to West Africa', the ship's combination steam reciprocating and turbine machinery drove the expresses at a mere 13 knots!

The Elder Dempster Line also operated two small capacity passenger ships, the *Tarkwa* and

The *City of Exeter* (1953) preparing to enter the Humber from the King George V Dock at Hull in July 1968.

The Union Castle Line's intermediate combination liner *Warwick Castle* (1938).　　　*Author's Collection*

Tamele, with accommodation for 40 saloon passengers and 32 students (36 students in the *Tamele*). They were diesel ships built at the end of the war and had modest service speeds of 13 knots. They maintained the regular service between Liverpool and Port Harcourt, and their accommodation was in big demand with West Africans studying away from home in Europe. They were both sold in 1966 for further service based out of Singapore.

The Ellerman & Bucknall Lines maintained a regular combination ship service from European ports (London, Hamburg, Antwerp, Hull and others on demand) to Las Palmas, Capetown, northwards to the South African coastal ports and on to Lorenco Marques (Maputo) and Beira. Four ships were built for this service by Vickers Armstrong at Barrow between 1952 and 1954. They were the *City of Port Elizabeth*, which entered service ahead of the other ships in January 1953, the *City of Exeter*, *City of York* and *City of Durban*. Each had accommodation for 107 first class passengers, who boarded the ship at Tilbury for

the 15-day voyage to Capetown. The public rooms were spacious and contained period furniture and valuable oil paintings, at least one of which was insured for £8,000.

The four *City* ships were very well patronised and to the end passenger bookings were always full at least three months in advance. In 1967 they were advertised to carry out a "series of short holiday voyages" to north continental ports, from Middlesbrough to Rotterdam and Hamburg and possibly also Antwerp, while the ships followed their normal loading programme, and with disembarkation at London. Eventually the passenger service was closed in June 1971 by the *City of York* and the four ships were then sold. Ellerman & Bucknall stated that unprecedented and massive rises in operating costs – bunkering, repairs and crew wages – was the reason for the withdrawal of the ships.

Services to the West African coast were maintained by the Union Castle Line, with their round-Africa service, and the direct services out of London via Suez also operated by

The intermediate cargo-passenger liner *Rhodesia Castle* (1951) passing through the English Channel at the start of a liner voyage   *Foto Flite*

Union Castle, with competition from British India. The Union Castle round-Africa service was the province of the sisters *Warwick Castle* and *Durban Castle* in post-war years. It survived only until 1962, when the ships were withdrawn and broken up. They had both been designed for the mail-ship service to South Africa, but had been transferred in 1950. The round-Africa service was never wholly a success in terms of passenger numbers. The *Warwick Castle* was originally named the *Pretoria Castle*. In 1942 she was stripped down to Main Deck level and converted to a flat-topped Auxilliary aircraft carrier. Her superstructure was completely refabricated after the war and was identical to her original build – save she lost the cabs at either side of the bridge.

Union Castle commissioned four post-war builds for the direct East Africa route. The first was the one-class emigrant ship *Bloemfontein Castle* (originally placed on the round-Africa service), which survived in the fleet for only nine years. The other three were the sisters

Rhodesia Castle, *Kenya Castle* and *Braemar Castle*. They had accommodation for 530 cabin class passengers and came from Harland & Wolff at Belfast in 1951 and 1952. They each received major refits in 1960 which included the provision of air conditioning in all cabins. The end came on 5 June 1967 when the Suez Canal was closed for the second time in ten years, on this occasion due to conflict between Israel and Egypt. The East African service was reduced to two ships (*Rhodesia Castle* and *Kenya Castle*) the previous year, but with Suez closed, re-routing via the Cape was no longer as viable as it had been when the canal was previously closed in 1956, and the other two ships were quickly disposed of.

The same fate awaited the British India Line East African service from London, which had been operated by the sisters *Uganda* and *Kenya*. These were the largest ships in the British India fleet (apart from the troopship *Nevasa*). They maintained the passenger and cargo service between London and ports such as Mombasa,

The *Leicestershire* (1949) in the West Float at Birkenhead, May 1963.

Tanga, Zanzibar, Dar-es-Salaam, Beira and Durban. They were completed in 1951 and 1952 by Barclay, Curle & Company at Glasgow, were equipped with turbine engines and had a speed of 16 knots. The *Uganda* and *Kenya* were two-class ships, with accommodation for 167 and 150 first class and 133 and 123 tourist class passengers respectively.

The *Kenya* and *Uganda* were better appointed than the one-class Union Castle ships, although the latter were perhaps less formal. The pair had cost £3 million to build and initially worked alongside the chartered Bibby Line's *Leicestershire*, which served on the East African route between 1950 and 1954 (see below). Only ten of the first class cabins in the British India Line ships were equipped with en suite facilities. The remainder preserved the ritual of being summoned by an Indian steward, bearing fresh white towels embroidered with the letters BISNCo, to a nearby bathroom with a huge steaming tub. The public rooms were extremely well appointed. The first class dining room aboard the *Kenya* sported a mural of Britannia and Aphrodite, and that of the *Uganda* a mural of London and Mombasa, this mural being later transferred to the main lounge aboard the *Canberra*. The *Uganda*'s smoke room was panelled in aspen and ash and there were carved panels which illustrated the use of tobacco as well as an African landscape. A gift from the Kabaka of Buganda, in the form of two elephant tusks, also adorned this room.

From January 1966 onwards, the British India service was run in collaboration with the Union Castle East African ships, with a monthly sailing in each direction. However, in 1967 the *Uganda* was withdrawn for conversion to an educational cruise ship (see Chapter 9) and the *Kenya* soldiered on, now as a one-class ship with berths for 297 passengers, and with the service terminating at Dar-es-Salaam. The *Kenya* arrived back in London for the last time in June 1969, leaving two weeks later for a breaker's yard in Spain.

The *Prome* (1937) riding high and at anchor.   *J & M Clarkson Collection*

Before the collaborative service began, there are many stories which illustrate the competition which existed between the two companies. On one occasion the *Kenya* was berthed adjacent to the *Kenya Castle* at Mombasa, and the British India boys managed to paint the slogan 'Ship and Travel by BI' along the starboard side of the Union Castle Line ship before she sailed. Revenge was sweet, as on the next contact of the two crews, a number of the toilets aboard the *Kenya* were quickly painted in Union Castle's lavender coloured paint, used on their ships hulls!

The long standing service between Glasgow and Birkenhead with Rangoon was operated jointly by the Bibby Line and the Henderson Line. Henderson Line maintained the two stately ships *Prome* and *Salween* on the route until their withdrawal in 1962. They were built by William Denny at Dumbarton in the late 1930s, and both went straight into war service, to serve in their own company colours only after the cessation of hostilities. They had

accommodation for 75 first class passengers, but ample deck space and public rooms meant that the passenger complement could be increased if demand warranted. They were single screw turbine ships with a service speed of 14 knots.

In the late 1950s, the Bibby Line maintained the Rangoon service with the *Worcestershire* and *Derbyshire* which were completed in 1931 and 1935 respectively, and the post-war built *Warwickshire* and *Leicestershire*. The older ships were originally four-masted and both had capacity for 115 first class passengers, reduced from an original pre-war capacity of 291. The *Worcestershire*, now a mainmast-only ship, was withdrawn and scrapped in 1961 and the now two-masted *Derbyshire* followed her in 1964.

The *Warwickshire* and *Leicestershire* were built in 1948 and 1949 respectively by the Fairfield Shipbuilding & Engineering Company. They were steam turbine driven ships because diesel engines were simply not available so soon after the war. Falling demand for passenger space,

HENDERSON LINE
TO PORT SAID · SUEZ · PORT SUDAN
ADEN · **RANGOON** & OTHER
BURMA PORTS

AGENTS FOR CARGO SERVICES TO
CALCUTTA · NEW ZEALAND

LONDON OFFICE
4 FENCHURCH AVENUE. E.C.3
TEL. MANSION HOUSE 4155

LIVERPOOL OFFICE
WELLINGTON BUILDINGS
TEL. MARITIME 2481

P. HENDERSON & CO.

R. BORLAND · A. G. McCRAE · A. S. HOUSTON · R. K. BORLAND
W. F. FULTON · J. W. K. HERBERTSON · A. BORLAND
SHIP MANAGERS · SHIP & INSURANCE BROKERS

Head Office
95 BOTHWELL STREET
P. O. BOX 22
GLASGOW C·2

TELEGRAMS CARTHAGE GLASGOW TELEX   TELEPHONE CENTRAL 8761
TELEX 77282

Our Ref. JMcW/AHS.   Your Ref.

10th August, 1962

N.S. Robins, Esq.,
  15, Brooklawn Drive,
     WITHINGTON,
        MANCHESTER 20.

Dear Sir,

        We thank you for your letter of 9th August and
have to advise you that indeed the "PROME" is on her last
voyage and will be going to the Shipbreakers at Bruges
about the end of September.

                Yours truly,

                    (signature)

        for STAFF SUPERINTENDENT

A letter to the author, in August 1962, confirming the last voyage of the *Prome*.

The *Caledonia* (1948) berthing at the Princes Landing Stage, Liverpool, to collect passengers for India, September 1963.

following the granting of independence to Burma in 1948, meant that the passenger complement of pre-war ships of about 250 was now superfluous. Consequently, they were designed to accommodate only 76 first class passengers in 28 single and 18 double berth staterooms, each with hinged windows and shutters on the Bridge Deck and four three-berth cabins on the Upper Deck. The main entrance and stairways were panelled (as Bibby Line tradition had it) in Burma teak, which the floors complemented in a rich blue colour. The public rooms included an 84-seater dining saloon, complete with a baby grand piano, and the lounge, which was at the forward end of the Promenade Deck, offered a grand piano and a mural depicting a hunting scene. There was also a smokeroom and cocktail bar on the Promenade Deck, each panelled in a variety of hardwood veneers. The Promenade Deck also offered a swimming pool and deck area for dancing, deck-tennis, quoits and skittles, plus the veranda café. The crew were part Indian and

Goanese, with British officers, seamen and engineers.

In the early 1960s both ships became cargo-only, before inevitable withdrawal and sale in 1965. The sisters were sold for conversion into the Mediterranean car ferries *Hania* and *Heraklion*, the latter (formerly the *Leicestershire*) foundering at sea with heavy loss of life in 1968. They had been distinctive looking ships with a pedigree that reflected the four-masted Bibby ships of former years.

In post-war years, the Glasgow and Liverpool to Bombay service of the Anchor Line was maintained by the *Circassia* and *Cilicia*, which were completed in 1937 and 1938 respectively, and the near sister-ship *Caledonia*, which was completed in 1948. Before the war the third ship was the *Britannia* which dated from 1926, and which was lost during the hostilities. The newer trio were all products of the Fairfield Shipbuilding & Engineering Company, with twin screws driven by Doxford diesels and a service speed of 16 knots. Combination liners,

The *Circassia* (1937) alongside the Princes Landing Stage, Liverpool, in October 1963.

they had traditional-style first class accommodation for 298 passengers (the *Caledonia* slightly more, with 304). The three ships maintained the Indian service throughout the 1950s, but during the 1960s suffered declining passenger numbers.

In August 1965 the Anchor Line was sold by its owners, the United Molasses Company Limited (then a subsidiary of the Tate & Lyle sugar group), to the Moor Line Limited of Newcastle-upon-Tyne for £2.35 million. The new owners stated that no change to the structure of the Anchor Line was envisaged. However, with the two older ships due for replacement, it was not surprising that the withdrawal of the service was planned for 1966, with the last outward sailing from Glasgow and Liverpool taking place in January. Both the *Cilicia* and the *Caledonia* maintained static roles in Holland for some years, but the *Circassia*, which had taken the final sailing, was sold for scrap on returning to the UK. Her sister *Cilicia* survived a further 15 years in her static

role as a training ship, before also being sold for demolition.

Hong Kong and Singapore were served by ships of the Peninsular & Oriental Steam Navigation Company, notably in post-war years by the *Carthage*, *Corfu* and *Canton*. The first pair were sister ships which came from the yard of Alexander Stephen & Sons in 1931, with accommodation for 181 first class and 213 tourist class passengers. The *Canton* followed from the same yard in 1938, with slightly larger passenger accommodation for 298 first and 244 tourist class passengers. All three had substantial cargo capacity. The *Carthage* and *Corfu* were displaced in 1961 by two second hand combination cargo and passenger liners. These were the Belgian ships *Badouinville*, the successor to the namesake that had earlier become the *Anselm* (see Chapter 4), and *Jadotville*, which became respectively the *Cathay* and *Chitral*. In addition to the Far Eastern ports served previously, the new ships continued on from Hong Kong to Yokohama

The *Cathay* (1957) departing from the Itchen Quays at Southampton in June 1969.

The *Chitral* (1956) arriving at Southampton during October 1968.

and Kobe, much as the old *Carthage* and *Corfu* had done in their early career. However, passenger traffic then on offer was not sufficient to retain the *Canton*, which had berths for 298 first class and 244 tourist class passengers, beyond 1962. She was then withdrawn and sold for breaking up.

The *Chitral* and *Cathay* continued on the route. They had been built in a Belgian and a French yard respectively, in 1956 and 1957. They had steam turbine machinery which drove them at just over 16 knots. The passenger accommodation provided for 240 in first class only. The passenger service continued throughout the 1960s, until the *Cathay* was withdrawn and transferred in November 1969 for further service with the Eastern & Australian Steamship Company in the Far East. Meanwhile, the *Chitral* was taken off the liner route early in 1970 and deployed in a series of cruises based at Genoa. These were not a success and the ship followed her sister to the Far East. The *Cathay* was only withdrawn (as the Chinese *Shanghai*) in 1996 and then only because she was unable to meet the new SOLAS regulations for safety of life at sea.

Passenger cargo liners to New Zealand were synonymous with the New Zealand Line. In 1960, the service was maintained via Panama with five ships. These included the elderly two-funnelled sisters *Rangitiki* and *Rangitata*, which were completed by John Brown & Company in 1929, and driven at 16 knots by Doxford diesels. The third sister, the *Rangitane*, fell victim to a German raider very early on in the war. As built, the *Rangitiki* (a misspelling of a New Zealand river) had a Georgian-style first class lounge, Tudor-style smoke room, and the first class drawing room was a reproduction of the style evolved by the Adam brothers. The dining room was Louis XIV! At that time they were the world's most powerful motor ships. Company tradition had it that the ship's master was never referred to as the captain, but always as the Commander.

The sisters had comfortable accommodation for 118 first class passengers in airy single and double berth cabins, on the Promenade and Bridge Decks. The 301 tourist class passengers were accommodated in cabins built on the Bibby principle on the Bridge, Main and Shelter Decks. There was also considerable refrigerated cargo space. On retirement, it was stated that the *Rangitata* had completed 144 passages through the Panama Canal, with total dues of some $1.5 million paid to the canal authority. The two ships had lasted until 1962 when they were replaced by a single ship, the *Remuera*, formerly the Cunard Line's intermediate ship *Parthia* (see Chapter 3). Not a success on the route, she was transferred to the Eastern & Australian Steamship Company in 1964, for whom she served until sold for demolition in 1970.

The three major post-war builds, which completed the five ship service, were the sisters *Rangitoto* and a new *Rangitane* which were completed in 1949, and the slightly smaller *Ruahine*, which was delivered in 1951. Together they cost £7 million to build. The larger ships had one-class accommodation for 436 passengers, and were the largest combination passenger and cargo ships in the British register, whereas the *Ruahine* could carry only 310. They were attractive ships, and to all intents and purposes looked like larger units of the cargo-only fleet of ships in the New Zealand Line and the associated Federal Steamship Company. The New Zealand Line adopted the latter company's attractive funnel colours in 1966.

The service was withdrawn in 1968–69, having lost money from the National Seaman's Union strike and the dockers' strikes. The latter had caused many departures from London to take place with a good passenger list but only part of the cargo loaded, before the scheduled departure date. Company chairman, Mr CAW Dawes said at the time:

These ships are following the path of many other such combination vessels – that is, ships

The *Ruahine* (1951) arriving at Southampton in August 1964.

which combine passengers with a substantial quantity of cargo space. It daily becomes more apparent that the passenger ship of today must be the type of ship that specialises almost entirely on the carriage of passengers, having sufficient cargo space only to carry passenger's baggage, mail and a small quantity of specialised cargo. The interests of running a rigid passenger schedule do not combine satisfactorily with those of a cargo service.

Following further service in the fleet of CY Tung, all three former New Zealand liners were broken up by 1976.

The other major British passenger cargo liner company operating to New Zealand was the Shaw Savill Line. The stalwart of the service was the *Dominion Monarch*, which carried 508 first-class-only passengers and was the company flagship. She had been completed in 1939 by Swan, Hunter & Wigham Richardson on the Tyne, and had Doxford diesels with quadruple screws which gave her a speed of over 19 knots.

She was displaced from the fleet in 1962 with the arrival of the new *Northern Star* (see Chapter 2).

Four new ships were commissioned in 1947 and 1948; these were the sisters *Athenic*, *Ceramic*, *Corinthic* and *Gothic*. The first pair were originally laid down as cargo liners, but when completed they all had accommodation for 85 first class passengers. There was a single suite and both single and double berth cabins. The *Gothic* was honoured in 1951 by being designated the royal yacht for the Commonwealth tour of King George VI, and although this voyage was cancelled, due to the declining health of the king, the ship was used in this role in 1953 by Queen Elizabeth. Both the *Athenic* and *Corinthic* were downgraded to cargo-only in 1965 and then sold for demolition in 1969. The *Gothic* was damaged by fire in 1968 and was subsequently broken up.

These three ships were replaced by the

The *Gothic* (1948) seen in the English Channel having just left London. *Foto Flite*

Akaroa, *Arawa* and *Aranda*, formerly of the Royal Mail Line. The three-class accommodation was revised to one-class only for 470 passengers and they maintained the round-the-world service, the *Akaroa* (ex-*Amazon*) in May 1968 and her two sisters a year later. This allowed the passenger-only ships *Southern Cross* and *Northern Star* to spend more time cruising. The service was short lived: the *Akaroa* was damaged by fire and withdrawn in 1970 and the other pair were also withdrawn the following year, the main problem seeming to be that their passenger capacity was too large to be economic on the route. Meanwhile, the faithful *Ceramic* had remained in service until 1972, but was then dispatched to the breaker's yard.

The closure of the Union Castle mail ship service to South Africa via St Helena in 1978 (originally by the *Capetown Castle* and latterly by the cargo liners *Good Hope Castle* and *Southampton Castle*, which then had

accommodation for 12 passengers) left the island without transport. A small, relatively young company, Curnow Shipping Limited purchased the former *Northland Prince* for £1 million in order to fill the gap. The purchase price was made with a loan from a London merchant bank, and alterations to the ship were financed by the British government. The ship had been built in 1963 in Vancouver for coastal service in the sheltered waters off British Columbia. Under the new name *St Helena*, and with accommodation for 76 passengers, she took up the service for the St Helena government, under the management of Curnow Shipping Limited (initially registered at London but later under the flag of St Helena), and under the ownership of the bank as security. A report in the *Pretoria News*, dated 1 November 1977, read:

> We very much hope we can follow in the wake of Union Castle. We are very much encouraged by the fact that in 1976

Safmarine and Union Castle carried just under 26,000 passengers between the UK and South Africa. If we fill every berth we have got to spare over the Island's need, we shall be after just over 3% of the passengers who travelled by sea last year.

The *St Helena* sailed between Avonmouth and Capetown calling at Jamestown in St Helena, and annually also at Tristan de Cunha. She made her inaugural voyage on the new service in December 1977, returning to Southampton for conversion work costing some £1.5 million, before next leaving Avonmouth via Las Palmas for the islands and Capetown on 13 September 1978. All cabins had portholes or windows with private bathroom facilities. There were two lounges on the Upper Deck, one with a small bar and a library. The dining saloon, shop and launderette were on the Main Deck.

The *St Helena* was requisitioned for service in the Falklands War as a minesweeper support vessel in 1982. She was temporarily replaced by

a former chemical carrier, the little *Aragonite*, built in 1958 as an explosives carrier, but which had 12 passenger berths, and later by the Blue Funnel Line's *Centaur* (see Chapter 6), and the Greek-owned *World Renaissance*. The latter ship offered a cruise itinerary known as the Cape Albion route as indeed she had 516 berths to sell in 220 cabins. The *World Renaissance* was not a success and was withdrawn from the route in March 1984, the *St Helena* having returned to the service in October 1983, after an absence of 16 months on war duties.

Curnow Shipping Limited looked at the *Centaur* (now registered at Singapore) with a view to purchase. However, decay of the aluminium superstructure and numerous mechanical problems that had surfaced during the charter made the company look to new building instead. This was arranged, and in due course Curnow retained management of new purpose-built tonnage for the route in the form of a second *St Helena*, this time registered in

The *St Helena* (1990) off the landing steps at Jamestown, St Helena, in August 1997.   *Henry Gunston*

Concentration on the bridge of the *St Helena* (1990) on approach to the anchorage at Jamestown.

Henry Gunston

London. The old *St Helena*, temporarily renamed *St Helena Island*, was sold on arrival of the new ship for further trading under the Maltese flag. The new ship was completed in Aberdeen in 1990; she was delivered eight months behind schedule and over budget by a reported £13 million, against the original estimate of £19 million. Her builders, Hall Russell, had gone into liquidation during her

construction, and the ship was completed under a new contract by A&P Appledore. The new *St Helena* has a capacity of 6,767 tons gross and can accommodate 132 passengers, 28 of them being so called 'inter-island' berths. She requires a crew of 58, the majority, apart from the officers, being from St Helena.

The aft end of the large Promenade Deck contains a swimming pool and sun lounge. Also on the Promenade Deck is a playroom and a quiet lounge. Below, on 'A' Deck, is a large lounge facing forward, and aft of this are some of the cabins each with their own en suite. The doctor's surgery, hospital and launderette are also on this deck. Other cabin accommodation, with adjacent bathroom facilities, is located on 'B' and 'C' Decks, and there is one four-berth cabin on the Promenade Deck. The purser's office and ship's shop are on 'B' Deck and the dining room and galley on 'C' Deck. The *St Helena* can carry 1,600 tons of cargo, including up to 62 standard 6 m containers, which are loaded through two hatches using the ship's own equipment. During cargo handling at St Helena, all through passengers are put ashore in a hotel for about eight days, while the ship does the shuttle run back to Ascension with workers from St Helena.

The *St Helena* is now Britain's one and only passenger liner, maintaining as she does the two monthly service between Cardiff and Capetown, via the islands of Ascension and St Helena. On the islands she is universally referred to as "the RMS". However, in 1992 and 1996 Curnow were put through the business of tendering for their own job, when the British aid agency (now the Department for International Development) decided to satisfy itself that Curnow was the cheapest and most effective way of delivering the requisite transport. Currently the *St Helena* sails via Tenerife and Ascension and calls annually at Tristan de Cunha. Her twin Mirrlees Blackstone oil engines provide a service speed of 14.5 knots. However, engine failure on the return leg of her maiden voyage required the charter of the former Royal Fleet Auxilliary landing ship *Lowland Lancer* to the service for a single round trip. Over the winter months of 1999–2000, she was again temporarily out of service at Falmouth, awaiting engine parts following a broken crank shaft. The small cruise ship *Jason*, owned by Royal Olympic, was chartered to complete the failed round trip.

Elder Dempster Line's *Aureol* of 1951

'The White Swan' and her two more functional contemporaries, the grey-hulled *Apapa* and *Accra*, maintained the fortnightly service between Liverpool and West Africa. The *Aureol* (named after a mountain in Sierra Leone) was the most attractive of the Elder Dempster Line combination passenger and cargo ships. The three ships were built following the loss of the *Abosso* and other passenger units in the war. The reverence with which Elder Dempster was held in those days is captured in the description of Christ as 'one time head-man, Elder Dempster Line'! Apart from catering for mainly first class clientele and cabin class, numerous deck passengers were also accommodated on the coastal voyages.

The passenger accommodation on the *Aureol* was spacious and luxurious. On the Upper Promenade Deck a special house accommodated the children's playroom and dining room. Below were two first class suites with sitting rooms opening out onto verandas, and aft of these was the first class swimming pool. There were spacious promenades either side of the Lower Promenade Deck, with the first class dance floor at the forward end. The Bridge Deck housed first and cabin class staterooms and the Upper Deck housed further cabin accommodation and the male and female hospitals. The dining saloons were on the Main Deck, with 275 seats in the first class and 100 seats in the cabin class saloons.

The public rooms were furnished with a variety of wood finishes, with blue upholstery and carpets piped with ivory. The lounge on the

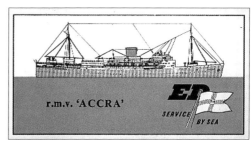
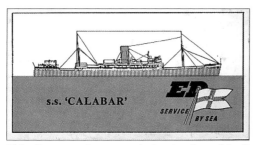

Elder Dempster cigarette cards showing four of the fleet.

Lower Promenade Deck was panelled in sycamore and ash, with large casement windows. This contained the obligatory grand piano, settees and armchairs and a screened area which opened on to the dance floor. Here the upholstery was rose and green. In addition, there was a well appointed library/chapel, smoking room and veranda cocktail bar. First class cabins consisted of single, double and two-plus-one staterooms, whereas cabin class had two- and three-berth staterooms also of a high standard, each with hot and cold running water. Only the first class saloon and the two hairdressing salons were air conditioned.

The ship was driven at 16 knots by two Stephen-Doxford oil engines, connected to twin propellers, each 4.8 m in diameter and weighing eight tons. There were also two Cochrane boilers which provided steam for a variety of purposes, and four diesel-driven generators which provided electricity. There were four holds, each serviced by electrically driven cranes and derricks. She carried both dry cargo and refrigerated goods.

The maiden voyage of the *Aureol* began on 8 November 1951, under the command of Captain JJ Smith. The three ships soon gained an enviable reputation for reliability and service, but by the mid-1960s passenger berths were less in demand, with independence being gained by the West African nations and the onset of air travel. In 1968 the *Aureol* adopted one class only, with revised accommodation for 451 passengers. The *Accra* and *Apapa* were withdrawn and she was left to maintain a departure every five weeks. She transferred to Southampton in 1972 to facilitate the faster service, but was finally withdrawn only two years later. Used subsequently only as an accommodation ship, she then lay rusting and at anchor until 2001 when she was finally sold for demolition.

6. The Ends of the Empire

A number of UK registered passenger ships traded entirely between foreign shores and only rarely came to the UK if a major refit or survey was due. These included the ships that plied the routes between India and Pakistan to the Middle East and Africa carrying migrant labour or bringing pilgrims to Mecca, principally via the Saudi Arabian port of Jeddah. The main UK operator was the British India Steam Navigation Company which employed 12 ships on wholly foreign trade routes in 1960. In addition, Alfred Holt had the former German East African Line steamer *Pretoria* deployed on the pilgrim trade between Indonesia and Jeddah under the name *Gunung Djati*. Other services operated by these two companies included the passenger, general cargo and cattle carrier *Centaur* on Alfred Holt's Blue Funnel Line service between Singapore and Freemantle, and the British India Line services between Asia and West Africa and between India, Singapore and Japan. Other overseas routes were operated by the Bank Line and the Austasia Line. However, all these passenger routes had ceased to operate by 1982 when the last of the ships, the British India Line's *Dwarka*, was finally retired.

The British India Steam Navigation Company was established in 1862 to connect Bombay and Calcutta with local and foreign trading destinations in the Indian Ocean. By 1914 it had become the largest British shipping company and had 131 ships. Amalgamation with P&O was arranged between the respective chairmen, Sir Thomas Sutherland and Lord Inchcape, creating a combined capital holding of £15 million. Retirement of the P&O chairman left Lord Inchcape in sole command of the combined assets.

The British India fleet was allowed to retain its separate identity. At the start of World War

The *Dwarka* (1947) seen in her original black hulled livery. Note the double-banked lifeboats typical of the high passenger capacity Indian Ocean ships. *P&O Steam Navigation Company*

Two it had 103 ships, of which 55 carried passengers; at the end of the war there were only 58 of the ships left afloat. British India also maintained significant workshop facilities at Mazagon Dock in Bombay and Garden Reach in Calcutta. A major post-war rebuilding programme was carried out, but the fleet never regained its former strength.

By 1960, the mainstay of the pilgrim and migrant labour trade were the 'D' Class sisters, *Dumra*, *Dara* and *Daressa*, which were built by Barclay Curle & Company on the Clyde in 1946, 1948 and 1950 respectively, and the *Dwarka* which came from Swan Hunter and Wigham Richardson's Tyneside yard in 1947. Principal routes operated by these ships were from Bombay and Karachi to the Persian Gulf where calls were made as required at Pasni, Gnadur, Muscat, Bandar Abbas, Shahjab, Dubai, Umm Said, Bahrain, Kuwait, Abadan, Khorramshahr and Basrah. The ships had diesel engines and could maintain a stately 14 knots. They had excellent first class accommodation for 13, and second class for 41 passengers, as well as plentiful unberthed passenger space – the *Dwarka* and *Daressa* could carry additional first and second class passengers subject to multiple cabin occupancy. The unberthed passengers were divided into three further classes.

The first class cabins on the *Dumra*, *Daressa* and *Dwarka* were on the Promenade Deck. There was a panelled foyer with a miniature grand stair-case, a comfortable dining saloon, a bar with the atmosphere of a backroom in a city pub, and a genteel lounge with writing desks and a small library. Each cabin had a window and was characteristically fitted out with dark furniture and at least three fans.

A fifth motor ship, the *Santhia*, dating from 1950, was also used on the Persian Gulf route. She was slightly smaller than the 'D' Class sisters but could accommodate 760 deck class passengers plus a further 268 passengers in what was described as 'bunked class'. She also had accommodation for 68 intermediate class

passengers, plus nearly 100 first and second class berths. This ship was sold for further service in 1967, but her auxiliary boilers failed in 1976 after which she was withdrawn and scrapped.

The greater number of those travelling were carried as deck passengers. The main visible sign of this extraordinary passenger capacity was the four double-banked sets of life boats stowed along the Boat Deck with three additional boats slung fore and aft of the central island. All four of the 'D' Class ships were certified to take over 1,000 unberthed passengers, and during the Haj they were normally full to capacity. Deck passengers provided their own catering using communal facilities, and in addition were content to entertain themselves in preparation for their visit to or return from Mecca. Migrant labourers, outward and return to the Middle East, were content to be at ease and to contemplate their futures during the voyage across the Indian Ocean. Temperatures on deck could, on occasion, reach the high 40s and in the days before air conditioning passengers were preoccupied with keeping cool.

Security in those days was virtually non-existent; certainly the airport-type security we know today was then unheard of. In any case, few believed that the ships were at risk, even though their popularity at some ports was at a low ebb at times, as the ships of the British India Line represented a former colonial ruler and more often than not brought unwanted or illegal immigrants to foreign ports. Notwithstanding, there was one very grave incident when the *Dara* was lost following an explosion caused by a terrorist bomb on passage from Basrah to Bombay on 7 April 1961. She had been unloading at Dubai when a violent storm forced her to leave the port and put to sea. In the early hours of the next morning, while she was returning to port, an explosion ripped through the 'tween decks and fire quickly took hold.

During the ensuing chaos 238 passengers, crew and Dubai shore workers died, both on board the *Dara* and in the sea. Another 581 survived, many being picked up by the British Tank Landing Craft *Empire Guillemot*, which had been pursuing the same course, there being no opportunity for the *Dara* to send out an SOS message before the radio room had to be abandoned. As the fire took hold, emergency power for fire fighting was not available and little could be done to dampen the flames. Passengers swarmed to the lifeboats, at least one of which overturned on reaching the water, while other people died of asphyxiation asleep in the 'tween decks. The last 15 men were taken off the stern of the *Dara* at daybreak when they were spotted by a ship's boat from the tanker *British Energy*.

When the master (Captain Elson had been taken from the water by the Norwegian registered *Thorsholm*) and a team of men reboarded the *Dara* on the second morning after the fire, it was obvious what had overcome the vessel. Gaping holes were apparent on the upper superstructure from the original explosion, but worse, charred bodies were found in the 'tween decks, and more were found in the companionways where men had been trapped as they clambered to the upper decks. The *Dara* was taken in tow by the tug *Ocean Salvor*, but she had been developing a list which increased to ten degrees, before the ship rolled on her side and settled on the shallow bottom, still attached to the tug. At the subsequent enquiry, the Wreck Commissioner, Mr JV Naisby, QC, decided that the fire had been deliberately started through the planting of a bomb aboard the ship. It was never proven who was responsible for this act of terrorism, but many believe to this day that it was probably Omani rebels, defeated by British forces only two years earlier.

The *Daressa* was sold shortly afterwards and again in 1964 to be transformed into a Greek flag cruise liner. This never materialised but she survived in the Far East until 1974 when her engines finally gave way. She was replaced on the Persian Gulf service by the *Sirdhana* which transferred from the Hong Kong and Japanese route in 1963. Competition from the air saw the *Dumra* withdrawn and broken up at Bombay in 1978, leaving the *Dwarka* to struggle on alone with a trade that was still very much in demand. Back in 1965 the first and second class accommodation aboard the *Dwarka* had been changed to saloon class, but she was still certified to carry 1,020 deck class passengers. The attraction of sailing in the *Dwarka* was that, unlike the airlines, she offered migrant workers to the Gulf unlimited baggage outwards and free carriage of their purchased consumer goods on the return trip. The end came when the airlines offered returning workers cut price rates for the carriage of their accompanied, but bulky luggage.

Her last master, Captain GA Hankin, took great pride in his ship. The ship had a crew of 132, mainly Indian and Goanese, with British officers. Captain Hankin spoke a number of local languages, and used to check for himself that his passengers were comfortable. In port, while the deck passengers boarded, a close watch was always kept by the purser for offensive weapons, while the ship's doctor watched for any sign of infectious diseases or advanced stages of pregnancies.

Although the *Dwarka* was a diesel ship, all of her auxiliary machinery was steam driven and this required two Scotch boilers to be kept in steam both at sea and in port. Major refit and alteration at the Kepple shipyard in Singapore converted some of the auxiliaries to electric operation, allowing her subsequent operating costs at sea to be reduced by about 25%. In this mode she survived until 1982 when she was sold for demolition in Pakistan, a final remnant of the British Empire, and for that matter the Indian Empire.

In 1960 the oldest member of the British India passenger fleet was the veteran *Rajula* built in 1926 on the Clyde, and only withdrawn

(Continued on page 77)

The elderly *Rajula* (1926) lying at anchor off Hong Kong in 1957. *P&O Steam Navigation Company*

The *Sangola* (1947) undergoing refit in February 1956 at the Hong Kong and Whampoa Dock Company in Hong Kong. *P&O Steam Navigation Company*

An impressive view of the *Aronda* (1941) at sea. *P&O Steam Navigation Company*

The *Karanja* (1948) seen at anchor off Hong Kong. *P&O Steam Navigation Company*

(Continued from page 74)
from company service in 1973. This ship maintained the service between Madras and Singapore with intermediate calls at Nagapattinam and Penang. This she did at a majestic speed of 12 knots. She was licensed in post-war years to carry 37 first class, 133 second class and 1,600 deck class passengers. But in the early part of her career she was certified to accommodate 5,000 passengers, by far the largest civilian passenger capacity of any British liner.

A service between Calcutta and Rangoon to Penang and Singapore, with onward calls at Hong Kong, Yokohama and Kobe in Japan was operated by the *Sangola* and *Sirdhana*, both sisters of the *Santhia* which operated to the Persian Gulf. This pair of ships maintained the combination of nearly 1,000 deck class and 335 bunked class passengers with just over 50 first class and second class berths. The service was withdrawn in 1962.

In addition, the steamer *Aronda*, which had been completed on the Tyne in 1941, ran between Karachi and Colombo and Chittagong. She had the normal first, second and intermediate class passenger capacity and could also carry 1,800 deck class passengers. She led an uneventful life until sold for breaking up, when she parted with her tug on the way to the breaker's yard and ended up on a Chinese beach.

On the African services were the sisters *Karanja* and *Kampala* (each built at a cost of £1.5 million in 1947–48) as well as the *Amra*, which was the older sister of the *Aronda* and dated from 1938. The India and Pakistan to Africa, and in particular South Africa, route had become important in the late nineteenth century. This was because the British government brought indentured labourers from India to work the sugar plantations of Natal. In later years many Indian merchants travelled to Africa – these people mainly came from the Gujarat province of north-west India.

The ships typically travelled between Bombay, Karachi and Mombasa, Dar es Salaam, Beira, Maputo and Durban, calling also at the Seychelles, although the *Amra* rarely ventured beyond Dar es Salaam. The *Amra* and *Aronda* were coal fired steamers (the third ship of this class, the *Aska*, was lost in 1940) although they were converted to oil burning once coal bunkering facilities at Durban were withdrawn. They offered up to 835 third class berths as well as accommodation for 73 first class passengers in 13 single berth staterooms, 29 double berth staterooms and one de luxe stateroom all arranged on the Bridge and Shelter Decks. The *Amra* also had accommodation for 62 second class passengers with separate ladies and gents washrooms distributed somewhat sparsely. Bunked and deck class were not available on these routes, although the ships could carry up to 2,300 deck passengers if required.

The *Amra* and *Kampala* were successively withdrawn in 1966 and 1971 and the *Karanja*, which had received a major refit at Singapore in 1969, closed the service in June 1976. In her final days with the British India Line she had accommodation for 60 first class, 180 second class and 800 'third' class passengers. She is reputed to have carried not one, but five ship's cats, each sponsored by a different crew member. The cats, by all accounts, were not at all partial to catching rats! As the Shipping Corporation of India's *Nancowry* she was only broken up in 1989.

The British India Line also had a small motorship maintaining their East African coastal service until 1961. This was the *Mombasa*, which had been built at Leith in 1950 and was of only 2,213 tons gross. This small vessel offered accommodation for 24 first and second class passengers and 250 deck class passengers. Originally there was a sister built for the service in 1951; this was the *Mtwara*, but the collapse of the infamous Tanganyikan Groundnut Scheme meant only one ship was needed and the *Mtwara* was sold to new owners in Saigon in 1953.

The baby of the British India Line fleet was the *Mombasa* (1950). She only carried the tropical white livery briefly in the 1950s before reverting to the more easily maintained black hull.   *P&O Steam Navigation Company*

The *Mombasa* was a veritable mini-liner, complete with a first class lounge, described as attractive and intimate, a first class saloon shared with the ship's officers, and a separate second class saloon. This accommodation, plus the cabins for first and second class passengers as well as the officers, was serviced by cool air from deckhead punkah-louvres. There were five separate galleys: two for unberthed passengers, two for the crew (their were 41 petty officers of various nationalities in the crew) and a European galley. Crew accommodation included cabins and dormitory style berthing, and the crew included the obligatory doctor, twelve servants, two wiremen and a Chinese fitter. It was not surprising that this large crew and meagre payload came under scrutiny as the coastal service began to run at a loss, the loss stated to relate to the progressive independence of some of the African nations from 1952 onwards. The *Mombasa* arrived at her namesake port for the last time in August 1960. She was

promptly sold to Indian flag operators, which she served for a further eight years before being scrapped.

Two other UK companies operated passenger ships on the India to South Africa route. One was Bullard, King & Company's Natal Line and the other was Andrew Weir & Company's Bank Line. In 1932 the Bank Line took over the Natal Line Indian service and brought out a trio of small but very well appointed passenger cargo liners. These were the *Inchanga*, *Isipingo* and *Incomati*, all named after geographical features in the Natal and Mozambique area. They were built by Workman, Clark at Belfast and could accommodate 50 first class and 20 second class passengers, and there was room for 500 unberthed passengers who were carried in the 'tween decks. The contrast between the classes was extreme. There was an entrance hall with shop and bureau on the Promenade Deck, and the lounge was decorated in Queen Anne style and opened out onto tea verandas either side. A

A rare picture of the *Gunung Djati* (1936) during trials on the Clyde in 1959 immediately after her conversion to a pilgrim carrier.   *Glasgow City Libraries and Archives*

smokeroom and veranda cafe overlooked the swimming pool on top of a cargo hatch. The engines on the *Incomati* were salvaged from the ill fated *Bermuda* which was lost by fire while at Belfast (see Chapter 8).

The first class accommodation was spacious and airy and had access to a large outdoor swimming pool. All first class cabins had windows and en suite facilities. The second class was accommodated aft. The ships had a gross tonnage of only 7,000, and were diesel powered. From 1934 until 1941 the service allowed a monthly departure from Calcutta to Capetown via Rangoon, Madras, Colombo, Mombasa, Beira, Lorenco Marques (Maputo) and Durban and Port Elizabeth. Passengers from Australia connected at Colombo, and passengers for the UK transferred to the Union Castle Line at Capetown. Only the *Inchanga* and *Isipingo* survived the war to restart the service in 1946. Although their passenger facilities remained intact, they were later reduced to a certificate for 12 passengers only, serving the route for a

further 18 years before they were both sold for demolition.

The Blue Funnel Line recognised the opportunity to use the troopship *Empire Doon*, later *Empire Orwell*, to good effect following her charter to an Indian company in 1958 for use in the pilgrim trade. Built in 1936 as the German liner *Pretoria*, she was ideal for conversion from trooping to a mass people carrier. However, she only survived three years as the newly converted *Gunung Djati* before being sold for many years active service under the Indonesian flag.

The Blue Funnel Line also maintained the express service between Singapore and Freemantle. In 1960 this was maintained by the small cargo passenger ships *Gorgon* and *Charon*, with one class accommodation for about 80 passengers and a service speed of only 14 knots. They were replaced in 1963 by a new build with increased capacity for 190 first class passengers in one, two and three berth cabins, plus two executive suites. This was the *Centaur*, which was built to withstand grounding when loading

Seen here during the war, the *Gorgon* (1933) was badly damaged by a Japanese bomb attack whilst delivering supplies to an Australian base in New Guinea in 1943. She was towed to Brisbane for repairs, and was only retired in 1963. *National Maritime Museum*

sheep and cattle, and which was heralded as an innovative ship with much to offer the future. Burmeister & Wain oil engines gave her a greatly enhanced operational speed of 20 knots.

Before starting on the service she undertook a trade mission for the Australian Chamber of Commerce. Thereafter she maintained a regular three weekly schedule between Freemantle and Singapore. Public rooms comprised two lounges, dining room, music room, shop and a children's playroom and play deck. There was a sheltered Sun Deck and a swimming pool. The ship was largely dependent on live sheep export from northern Australia (cattle also in season) and passengers, which included workers returning to Malaysia for leave periods, as well as people travelling on business. Pens were available for up to 4,500 sheep and 700 cattle. Air was circulated through the animal decks at 30 changes per hour and the spent air was emitted through the mast heads (which were unusually thick) and the funnel top.

From 1973 onwards the *Centaur* was flagged overseas. However, she returned to UK registry throughout 1983 when she acted as an interim vessel for the UK to St Helena and Capetown service for Curnow Shipping Limited, but was sold to Chinese interests in 1986. Perhaps her greatest claim to fame is that she was the last British passenger liner built specifically to service a route that had no UK terminal – this was indeed the end of the Empire.

The final effort in this passenger trade was the introduction of the former Booth Line ships *Hubert* and *Anselm* (see Chapter 4) on the Austasia Line service between Singapore and Malaya to Australia in 1964. The ships were renamed *Malaysia* and *Autralasia* respectively. The passenger service remained on offer until 1976 when container ships were introduced.

Gunung Djati

One of two sisters built for the German East Africa Line express passenger and cargo service, the *Pretoria* was completed by Blohm & Voss in 1936. The *Pretoria* and her sister *Windhuk* were of 16,662 gross tons and could maintain a service speed of 18 knots. They were designed very much with direct competition to the Union Castle Line in mind. However, after only thirteen round trips the *Pretoria* returned to Hamburg and spent an uneventful war largely as an accommodation ship. At the end of the hostilities she was taken as a war prize and assigned to Britain under the Tripartite Commission. She was sent to the Tyne for conversion to the troop carrier *Empire Doon* and put under the management of the Orient Steam Navigation Company.

Significant engine problems arose and a major refit followed, costing some £2 million. She emerged in 1947 under the new name of *Empire Orwell* (in keeping with the Orient Line 'O' nomenclature) with capacity for 1,491 troops. Following a single voyage to Egypt she settled down into a regular run between Southampton, Singapore and Hong Kong. At the end of this she was chartered to the Pakistan Pan-Islamic Steamship Company in 1958, given a Clan Line crew and that year served the pilgrim season between Karachi and Jeddah. On return to the UK she was bought by the Blue Funnel Line and renamed *Gunung Djati* after an Islamic missionary.

Blue Funnel had long carried pilgrims to Mecca on their regular services, and had converted the elderly *Tyndareus* into a pilgrim ship in 1949 with space for 2,500 passengers. Built in 1916 and powered by steam reciprocating machinery, this 11,346 gross ton steamer could maintain only 13 knots. The *Gunung Djati* was her successor. Conversion for full time use in the pilgrim trade was undertaken by Barclay, Curle. She then had first class accommodation for 106 and space for 2,000 pilgrims. The conversion included the provision of a mosque, an outdoor cinema used for religious films, special galley facilities and arrows which pointed to the east to assist in prayer. The arrows were under the charge of a midshipman and were mechanically, but separately, connected along the port and starboard sides of the ship. The Mullah was never aware that they did not all point in the same direction all of the time!

After only four years with the Blue Funnel Line, the ship was taken over by the Indonesian government but still maintained in the pilgrim trade. She was re-engined in 1973, when her original turbines were stripped out and diesel machinery was installed. She later saw service as an Indonesian troopship and a military accommodation ship, before being sold for demolition in 1987. Meanwhile, her sister ship the *Windhuk* had been laid up by the US Navy and was broken up in 1966.

7. The 12s, 18s and 30s

Authority to carry up to 12 passengers at sea is open to any carrier. It has always been seen as a means of turning a penny, and 40 years ago many of the cargo liners of the day had facilities, usually of a very high standard, to carry 12 passengers. The practice has diminished today. Vessels varied from the small freighters of the MacAndrews fleet on the relatively short journeys to and from Spain and Gibraltar (with both single and twin berth cabins on offer aboard most of their ships) to the fast cargo liners of the Ben Line or Alfred Holt's mighty fleet of cargo liners on the Far Eastern services. By way of example the Glen Line's *Flintshire*-class of 1960 offered a Promenade Deck exclusively for the 12 passengers (there was a crew of 70) and a large attractive lounge. The dining room, which was shared by the ship's officers, was on the Bridge Deck. The passengers were accommodated in two suites with day room, bedroom and bathroom, or four double-berth staterooms.

The Ben Line's *Benloyal*-class, dating from the late 1950s, offered three double and six single-berth cabins on the Boat Deck with furnishings selected by one of the company director's wives. The passengers' lounge and smoke room were situated on this same deck, with a 33 seater dining saloon at the after end of the Bridge Deck. They had a service speed of 20 knots and could complete the voyage between London and Singapore in 19 days. Alas, containerisation saw their premature end in the early 1970s.

Other liner companies offering good quality accommodation for 12 or sometimes only 8 passengers included the Blue Star Line, Port Line, Prince Line, Manchester Liners, Henderson Line, Jamaican Banana Producers, Elder Dempster and Union Castle.

In the 1940s the Blue Star Line gave three of its cargo ships significantly more passenger accommodation to satisfy the immediate post-war demand. The first was the *Empire Mercia* which became the *Empire Star* in 1946 and had room for 36 first class passengers in four-berth, three-berth and two-berth cabins in a deck house at the forward end of the Bridge Deck, and 96 tourist class passengers in two, four, six and eight-berth cabins fitted into the Bridge 'Tween Decks. She reverted to 12 first class passengers only in the early 1950s, and remained in the fleet until 1971. The other pair were the *South Africa Star* and *Rhodesia Star* which joined Blue Star Line in 1948 with accommodation for 26 passengers. They had been built in 1943 as American standard C3 ships but were completed by the US Navy as the escort carriers USS *Reaper* and the USS *Estero*, becoming HMS *Winjah* and HMS *Premier* respectively, on transfer to the Royal Navy under the Lend-Lease agreement. Their passenger accommodation was also reduced in the 1950s.

Few British cargo ships have offered passenger accommodation in recent years. There are some exceptions and these have included trips to the Gulf and Indian ports served by the Bank Line's *Forthbank* and *Clydebank* in the 1990s, although the ships themselves were respectively built in 1973 and 1974. Accommodation on these ships consisted of four twin-bedded cabins, one of which was the owner's suite, and one single cabin. Each was spacious and equipped with all manner of services and comforts. The passengers' lounge was aft on the same deck as the cabins and had three sides made of glass to provide panoramic views (the lounge was obviously referred to by the crew as the aquarium!). The cost of these trips was about $100 per day.

Carriage of more than 12 passengers needs special certification and requires the ship to carry a doctor. In 1910 the Blue Funnel Line, Ocean Steamship Company commissioned three ships

The *Helenus* (1949) manoeuvring in the Langton Dock at Liverpool in March 1967.

The *Ixion* (1951) viewed from the air – note the narrow and pointed forward hold.   *John Shepherd Collection*

Blue Funnel Line's 'P' class steamer *Peleus* (1949) passing Gibraltar.   *John Shepherd Collection*

to carry cargo and 170 first class passengers. They were followed by the four-ship *Sarpedon*-class in 1923–24 which could carry 155 passengers on the route from Liverpool via Suez to Aden, Colombo, Penang, Singapore, Manila, Hong Kong, Shanghai, Kobe and Yokohama. The *Sarpedon*, built in 1923, and *Antenor*, built in 1925, alone survived the war, and were put back into service with accommodation for only 48 and 39 first class passengers. Other surviving passenger units in the Blue Funnel Line fleet were the elderly *Ascanius* and the *Nestor*, both withdrawn and scrapped by 1950.

A series of eight ships with limited passenger accommodation were ordered in rapid succession by the company to replace the war losses for the cargo passenger services to Australia and the Far East. They were based on an earlier design used for eight *Glenroy*-class ships completed before the war and two *Priam*-class ships completed during the war. The four ships for the Australian service were the *Helenus*, *Hector* and *Ixion*, which came from Harland &

Wolff at Belfast between October 1949 and January 1951, and the *Jason* which Swan Hunter delivered in January 1950. They had a larger refrigerated cargo space than the ships on the Far East route, and there was an extra hold and forward hatch. However, the forward hold was so pointed by the fine lines of the ships that they were a headache to chief officers in charge of cargo loading for the ensuing 20-odd years of the ships' careers.

The four ships built for the Far Eastern trade were the *Peleus* and *Pyrrhus*, which were delivered in March and August 1949 by Cammell Laird, along with the *Perseus* and *Patroclus* which were delivered by Vickers Armstrong on the Tyne in April and February 1950. They each had a gross tonnage of around 10,100. They were equipped with steam turbine engines even though tenders for their construction included an option for diesel machinery. However, with a design speed of 18 knots, appropriate diesel machinery was not available in this immediate post-war period. The turbines consumed some 82 tonnes of fuel oil per day at 18 knots. Downdraft from the funnel posed a problem with soot falling on the after deck and blackening of the superstructure; this required some later modification to the funnels. All of these fast and prestigious vessels were dry docked, and all machinery fully serviced on each UK return, so ensuring a mechanically reliable service.

Passenger accommodation was almost identical in each ship. There were 17 passenger cabins with a total of 29 berths, and they were all situated on the Promenade Deck. There was also a two-berth cabin available for Chinese 'amahs', or nannies, travelling with European families on the Far East run. Also on the Promenade Deck was a small cocktail bar and a large observation lounge facing forward. The dining room was shared with the ship's officers. The Promenade Deck offered shaded areas and open sun deck areas, and a portable swimming pool could be erected forward of the main superstructure.

The Australian service was a huge success and was based on a monthly departure from Birkenhead. The Far Eastern service ran into trouble from an early stage, a combination of the Korean War and the communist take over of Chinese port administration meaning that the 'P' class ships had to turn at Japan without going on to mainland China. Nevertheless, a departure from Birkenhead was scheduled for the thirteenth day of each month, and after calling at Rotterdam, the ships sailed for Suez and the Far East.

The spirit of the day is summarised in this letter from Chris Adams, now with Research Vessel Services at Southampton:

You mention the P & H classes. I served on both the *Pyrrhus* and *Ixion* – amazing vessels. Both of these classes used to get priority in the Suez Canal convoys as they were (usually) carrying Royal Mail for the garrisons in Singapore and Hong Kong – plus sundry War Office or diplomatic vehicles (several Ambassadorial Rolls Royces and armoured cars) or bullion and jade in bulk. One voyage from the Far East to Liverpool on the *Pyrrhus*, we had the Commodore Master on his final (retiring) trip, and he gave orders as we left Port Said for the Chief Engineer to "Put on 26 nozzles on the boilers", the term used to maximise the turbine power.

We arrived in Gladstone Lock with only a scoopful left in the bunker tanks, having used over 1,500 tonnes of fuel between bunkering in Aden and arrival in Liverpool. The Old Man got a rollicking for that from the company, but we overtook a P & O liner plus an American Lines superfast (for that period) cargo boat and felt it was justified. As the Old Man stood on the Monkey Island shaking his fist at them, we had zoomed past in a huge pall of black smoke from our very hot funnel.

It was on that trip that the *Queen Elizabeth* crossed our bows in thick fog outbound to New York, and we only saw her at a range of about 5 cables as her after mast briefly appeared in the fog. We hit her wake at full tilt and reared up in the air. So much for prudent speed in fog – both ships were going flat out. It was almost a case of changing trousers!

Competition from the air induced the 'de-passengerisation' of the eight ships in 1961 and 1962. This amounted to a reduction in the number of catering crew and the expansion of the officers and petty officers accommodation to include the former passenger spaces. Overtaken by the move to containerisation, they were all successively withdrawn in 1972 and 1973. The only major mishap to happen to the octet was fire aboard the *Pyrrhus* at Liverpool in November 1964. This was extinguished by sinking the ship at her berth, but the subsequent renovations cost her two round trips to the Far East.

A number of the Blue Funnel Line's so called A-Class ships built in the post-war years were equipped to carry several hundred pilgrims during the Haj. All of this class had excellent accommodation for 12 passengers, but a group of them (the *Antilochus, Autolycus, Automedon, Clytoneus* and *Cyclops*) differed in that they had

The Blue Funnel Line's *Antilochus* (1949) on a charter to the Elder Dempster Line. She normally carried only 12 passengers but was one of a number of ships equipped to carry pilgrims during the Haj.

portholes in the 'tween decks and the centre castle beneath the main superstructure. In addition, facilities were provided for cooking and sanitation, along with appropriate lighting and ventilation. Additional life boats were carried when this accommodation was in use. The carriage of pilgrims ceased in 1958 when the *Gunung Djati* took over the trade (see Chapter 6).

Glen Line, also part of the Alfred Holt Group, offered accommodation for 18 passengers in eight of its fast cargo ships. Regulations insist that the extra six passengers over the normal 12 require that a ship's doctor be carried. Could this have been one of the easiest jobs in the medical profession? The eight ships included the *Glenroy*, precursor to the 'P' and 'H' Blue Funnel Line ships and her seven sisters built between 1938 and 1942. The Glen Line ships were equipped with Burmeister and Wain diesels which gave them a service speed of 17 knots. The Caledon Shipbuilding & Engineering Company built the *Breconshire, Glenartney, Glenearn, Glengyle* and

Priam; the *Denbighshire* came from the Netherlands Shipbuilding Company in Amsterdam; the *Glenroy* herself from Scotts Shipbuilding & Engineering on the Clyde; and the *Glengarry* from Burmeister & Wain at Copenghagen. When Denmark was overrun by the Germans, the *Glengarry* was seized and completed as the German raider *Meersburg*, and later used as the cadet training ship *Hansa*. She was recaptured in 1945 – Captain FA Brown received orders from Mr Lawrence Holt "to take a party of engineers to Hamburg, protect the Company interests, and bring back the former *Glengarry* in one piece". She was found lying in Kiel Roads and although much altered, Captain Brown wrote: "The shape of the bow, the navigating bridge, the funnel and the counter all added up to *Glengarry*; and for good measure the name, chisel-cut into the stern plating was discernable even under the paint."

On return to the UK the ship was at first considered a naval prize, having never served her owners, and so she became the *Empire Humber*

The *Glengarry* (1940), her war-time exploits long behind her, seen from the air in the early 1960s.   *Foto Flite*

for the British Ministry of Transport before being taken back by the Glen Line. The ship had been confined to port at Southampton with an Admiralty writ pinned to the captain's cabin door (the steel mast had been too unremitting for this purpose). Orders received from head office conflicted with the Admiralty instruction and loyal to his employers rather than the Admiralty, Captain Brown hove anchor.

> No shots passed across our bows as we steamed (sic) through the Needles Channel, and as we had no pilot we did not stop. From that day on I have heard no more about my infringement of Maritime Law. I assume my delinquency was overlooked in the confusion of those days; or perhaps the Master of some other *Empire Humber* (believed to be a tug!) is still in gaol.

The eight ships settled into civilian life to maintain the Glen Line service to Malaya, Hong Kong, China and Japan from both British and north European ports. The *Priam* was renamed *Glenorchy* on transfer from the Blue Funnel fleet in 1948. The ships were reduced to 12-passenger status in 1964, except for the *Glengarry* which then ceased to carry passengers at all. They were successively withdrawn and scrapped over the next few years, some passing into Blue Funnel ownership in the meantime.

None of the other post-war UK ship operators offered these small passenger complements on what were essentially cargo liners. With the ending of the Blue Funnel and Glen Line passenger facilities in the early 1960s went a unique form of luxury travel. Although a number of liner companies still offered passenger accommodation for eight or 12 passengers for some years, these are now rare and the few liner voyages that are still available are in strong demand.

8. Early Cruise Ships

An increasing interest in day excursion steamers, the so called summer 'Butterfly Boats', on the Thames, Clyde and elsewhere, was developing during the Victorian and Edwardian eras. Liner companies were conscious of this and there were a number of notable developments whereby liners were deployed on cruises between scheduled voyages. Amongst the earliest successful regular cruises were the Union Line 'Yachting Cruises' to Hamburg, Antwerp and Rotterdam, which started in 1894 from Southampton. These were continued by the Union Castle Line until 1914. In 1904 the *Dunvegan Castle* also made several trips to Norway, the Mediterranean and round Britain. In this same year P&O put the *Vectis* on a programme of ten cruises 'Carrying passengers round a given route, calling at various ports and bringing them back to their port of embarkation'. The 'cruise yacht' *Vectis* carried up to 180 passengers on trips to the Baltic and Norway, the Holy Land, Constantinople and the Adriatic, the Canaries and Algiers.

Cruising, or in truth, cruising to and from a holiday destination, was provided with a great incentive by the introduction of Prohibition in the United States in 1919. Just as the American Matson Line developed 'booze cruises' to the company-owned Royal Hawaiian Hotel during the 1920s, so Furness Withy developed cruises to company-owned hotels in Bermuda. Furness Withy had previously introduced a three-ship service between New York and Bermuda after the Great War, when they acquired the Quebec Steamship Company and their interests. These included the steamer *Bermudian*, which was renamed *Fort Hamilton* in 1919, and which was fitted out with first class accommodation. At the same time they also bought the *Willochra* and *Wandilla* from the Adelaide Steamship Company and renamed them *Fort Victoria* and *Fort St George*, and took over large interests in hotels on the 'holiday isle' of Bermuda.

The company commissioned a purpose-built luxury liner in 1927, the *Bermuda*, with berths for 616 first class passengers. The new ship replaced the *Fort Hamilton*. The target customer was the very rich and well to do. A consort for the *Bermuda* was commissioned shortly afterwards, but in 1930 the *Fort Victoria* was sunk in collision. Before the second ship was completed, the *Bermuda* suffered two separate incidents in which fire destroyed large parts of the ship. The Cunard Line's *Carinthia* was hastily chartered to run alongside the *Fort St George*.

The consort was the magnificent three-funnelled liner *Monarch of Bermuda*, built by Vickers Armstrong at the Walker yard on the Tyne. Her arrival allowed the *Fort St George* to be disposed of. The *Monarch of Bermuda* was so successful on the route that a sister, the *Queen of Bermuda*, followed from Vickers the following year, this time from their yard at Barrow. She was the only large merchant ship to be completed in 1932–33 (the *Queen Mary* was silent on the stocks on the Clyde at that stage of the Great Depression). The ships were registered at London under the ownership of the Furness Bermuda Line. They were designed with the narrow harbour at Hamilton in mind, and were consequently short for their tonnage and of shallow draught. Manoeuvrability was enhanced by using turbo-electric drive with direct control from the bridge, coupled to four propellers.

The pair were essentially first class luxury liners and the décor was a mixture of Art Deco and a gentleman's club. There was a small second class area aft, principally used by Bermudan residents. The two ships maintained a twice weekly departure from Piers 95–97 at New York, disembarking passengers into tenders at St

The *Queen of Bermuda* (1933) undergoing trials on the Clyde before being handed over to her owners.

The Sankey Collection

George en route to the company hotels. The ships then proceeded to Hamilton to discharge up to 2,000 tons of fresh water, frozen goods and the odd race horse or two.

Both ships spent the war trooping. In the immediate post-war refurbishment programme fire struck again when the *Monarch of Bermuda* was declared a constructive total loss after being gutted at Belfast. She was towed away to the Fal to await her fate. With the shortage of ships at that time, she was taken over by the Ministry of Transport and rebuilt as the immigrant ship *New Australia* (see Chapter 3), later becoming the Greek Line's *Arkadia* before going to the scrap yard in 1966.

Shortly afterwards the *Queen of Bermuda* returned to service with her three funnels no longer the same height but stepped down from fore to aft. In time, her third dummy funnel was removed and in 1962 a new and rather ugly single funnel was installed along with new boilers, an air conditioning plant and a new

streamlined bow section. With the loss of the *Monarch of Bermuda*, another consort was required, and in 1951 the *Ocean Monarch* was commissioned, also from Vickers Armstrong. She had a smaller passenger capacity of 438 first class against the *Queen*'s post-war complement of 733. The new ship ran a cruising programme to the Caribbean in the off-season, but the *Queen of Bermuda* remained on the Bermuda run. Marketing increasingly recognised that Bermuda was no longer the preserve of the very wealthy, and in the late 1950s a return fare to Bermuda started at only $153. The *Ocean Monarch* was given a flume stabiliser in 1963, when some additional cabins were also installed on the Promenade Deck.

Competition from the air, increasing running costs – particularly the price of fuel oil – plus increasingly stringent US Marine safety regulations led inevitably to the withdrawal of the service in 1966. The *Ocean Monarch* was sold for further service. For a short while the Cunard liner *Franconia* (see Chapter 2) stepped into the breach to maintain the New York to Bermuda service, but alas this was short lived. In 1970 it was even reported that the Furness Group were negotiating with Vickers Limited at Barrow-in-Furness for a small cruise liner to maintain the Bermuda crossing in season and to be deployed elsewhere for the remainder of the year. Sadly, no contract was ever placed.

The *Queen of Bermuda* coincidentally arrived at the breaker's yard in the same month that her sister, now the *Arkadia*, also went under the torch. Incredibly, the *Ocean Monarch*, now renamed *Varna* by the Bulgarian State Shipping Enterprise (they were going to call her *Reina del Mar* at one stage!), later renamed the *Riviera* under the Greek flag, was destroyed by fire while refitting at Perama in 1981. The curse of the 'booze, sex and sun' ships was unforgiving, with only the *Queen of Bermuda* and two of the three *Forts* managing to escape destruction by fire or loss at sea.

The Depression of the 1930s caused a number of companies to look to cruising. The shipping industry had become an early victim of the Wall Street Crash, and although most transatlantic services were maintained through 1931, albeit with considerable losses, many sailings were withdrawn in 1932. Ships were dispatched to lay up in Scottish lochs and river estuaries, others lay in dock with canvas covers over their funnels, while some were sold as they lay to the breakers for as little as £1 per ton. For others the role of cruise ship became a lifeline – there were even cruises aimed at children and Boy Scouts for as little as £1 per day.

A number of magnificent ships took up this new career including the majestic Lamport & Holt liner *Vandyck*. Services were leisurely – the 1931-built Canadian Pacific Line's *Empress of Britain* had two of her four propellers removed prior to becoming a cruise ship. Another company which took up cruising in earnest was the Blue Star Line, which had built five 'A' class passenger cargo liners in the late 1920s as a means of gaining entry to the South American Conference. However, in 1929, the *Arandora Star* (first commissioned under the name *Arandora*) was converted at a cost of £200,000 for use as a dedicated cruise ship with capacity for 350 passengers. In this role she was extremely successful and very popular. For the next ten years she made a wide range of cruises including brief one day cruises off the south coast and more substantial cruises to Norway, the Mediterranean, the Caribbean and the Pacific. Sadly the ship was torpedoed in the war with the loss of 805 lives in July 1940.

Another company that adopted cruising was the Royal Mail Steam Packet Company who converted one of their five 'A' Class liners, the 1913-built *Andes*, into a luxury cruise liner at the start of the slump in 1929. As such, she could carry 450 first class passengers. Cruising destinations typically included ports in northern Europe, the Mediterranean or the Caribbean, but she also went on longer cruises to South Africa and to South America, sometimes also via the Panama Canal to Hawaii and the Pacific Islands.

Even the Southern Railway cross-channel steamer *St Briac* took part in a seasonal cruise programme throughout much of the 1930s. Cruising had become a lifeline to ship owners, much as it was again going to be in the 1960s and 1970s.

A number of liner companies began to build ships with a view to cruising on a part-time basis. Perhaps the most innovative of these was the Orient Line's *Orion* (see Chapter 3) which was delivered by Vickers Armstrong at Barrow and launched in December 1934. A junior director, Colin Anderson, then only 29 years old and a member of the majority shareholding family of the Orient Line, was instructed to oversee the design and construction of the new ship. Anderson, in turn, commissioned a 32-year-old New Zealander, Brian O'Rorke, to design the interiors. The ship attracted the new corn-coloured livery of the company and was unique

The Southern Railway steamer *St Briac* (1924) was the first of a number of railway-owned ferries to masquerade as a seasonal cruise ship before and after World War Two.   *Mike Walker Collection*

as she carried only one mast. Her public rooms abandoned the dark wooden baronial halls and pseudo-Victorian effects of contemporary liners, instead adopting light panelling, wooden flooring and plentiful use of rugs. Curtain drapes and fireplaces were completely out. In addition, there was no third class, this being replaced with tourist class, which was considerably more comfortable and even included a swimming pool and passenger lift.

The initial schedule for the *Orion* included two return trips to Australia during the winter months and a summer season spent cruising as a first-class-only vessel. The summer cruises of the 1930s included a Southampton-based cruise to the Mediterranean and north European cruises, the latter based on the port of Immingham. Her younger sister *Orcades*, which also undertook seasonal cruises, was lost in the war.

In post war years, Cunard was quick to take up cruising out of New York, but very few other liner companies were then interested in the cruise market. This slowly changed as more and more liners found earning a living on their design route an increasingly difficult challenge. Although a number of companies (including Cunard) converted liner tonnage to a dual purpose cruising role, others, such as the Royal Mail Line, converted to full-time cruising (see below).

The Cunard experience illustrates how liner tonnage slowly took on the dual role. The early career of the *Mauretania* was spent at war, after only five months civilian service. Once hostilities had ceased, it quickly became clear that she was to operate on a cruising schedule during the winter months, commencing in January 1948 with five 14-day cruises from New York to the Caribbean. These were the first winter Cunard White Star cruises for eight years, and this became the pattern for the ship for the remainder of her career. Her first cruise to the Mediterranean took place in February 1962, also from New York. That same year she was painted in a distinctive cruising green livery. In 1964 she took up a cruising programme from

The *Mauretania* (1939), resplendent in Cunard's cruising green livery at Ocean Dock, Southampton.

Southampton, but her final voyage was again from New York terminating at Southampton in November 1965.

The *Mauretania*'s main cruising partner at New York was the *Caronia*. In the early days it was not uncommon for passengers to turn up at the quayside with 17 pieces of baggage, wardrobe trunks and ladies' fur coats for the cold store aboard ship! The *Caronia* was the first Cunard ship to be designed for the dual role; she was intended for cruising for much of the year but was also capable of serving on the North Atlantic crossing. She was launched in October 1947 in the cruising green colours; her accommodation was organised between 528 first class and 332 tourist class passengers. Most cruises started and finished at New York, attracting valuable dollars for her owners. However, throughout her career she was dogged with mechanical problems, particularly her turbine gearing.

The same green livery was given to the intermediate liners *Saxonia*, when she was renamed the *Carmania*, and the *Ivernia*, which became the *Franconia*, following a major refit in 1963. The refit cost £2 million and included the provision of a Lido Deck and swimming pool plus other features expected of a warm weather cruise ship. Although retained on the Canadian service in summer, they were then put on a winter cruise schedule. There were one or two problems: the *Carmania* ran foul of the United States government in December 1968 when they refused to accept her UK Board of Trade Certificate. Rapid internal modifications enabled her to fulfil her next cruise, but only to run aground on the Bahama Banks on 13 January 1969. On refloating, repairs were put in hand at Newport News.

The *Sylvania* and *Carinthia* (see Chapter 2) were also upgraded for off-season cruising in the winter of 1963–64. Even the *Queen Elizabeth* was dealt with in this manner two winters later. It was also announced that the proposed replacement for the *Queen Mary* (the *Queen Elizabeth 2*) would be designed, like the *Caronia* before her, as a dual purpose liner and cruise ship.

(Continued on page 94)

The *Carmania* (1954), in cruising green, arriving back at Southampton Itchen Quays in August 1964.

The *Franconia* (1955), seen in her all white livery at Southampton in November 1969.

The *Orcades* (1949), seen in P&O-Orient all white livery at Southampton in July 1969.

(Continued from page 92)

The *Sylvania* (now in all white livery) and *Carinthia*, along with the *Caronia*, were withdrawn and sold in 1968. The *Caronia*, subsequently renamed *Columbia* and then *Caribia*, only undertook a few cruises for her new owners. Sold for demolition in 1974, she foundered at Guam while being towed to the breaker's yard in Taiwan. She heeled over to 70° and rapidly broke into three pieces. The *Queen Elizabeth* completed her final voyage for Cunard also in 1968, and she too met with a violent end (see Chapter 2). The *Franconia* and *Carmania* were eventually laid up in 1971, when Cunard suggested that they should be partially crewed by foreign personnel. Unable to reach agreement over manning scales with the National Union of Seamen, the two ships were put up for sale. However, all of these ships had proved successful in their dual roles.

The ultimate dual role ship must be the former British troopship *Dilwara* (see Chapter 9), which became the China Navigation Company's *Kuala Lumpur*. In this role, albeit considerably updated since her career as a troopship, she worked the pilgrim run to Jeddah for the Haj and off-season she conducted cruises out of Australia.

Other ships were converted for use entirely as cruise ships. One such was the Royal Mail Line's *Andes*, which was refitted in 1960 at Flushing. Work included the removal of all cargo spaces, rebuilding of accommodation and the fitting of air conditioning throughout. Another major refit took place in 1969. She was targeted at an exclusive clientele and even developed her own fan club, the 'Andes Cruise Club'. Her crew of 500 tended on the demands of only 480 cruise passengers. However, engine problems put an end to her career and she was withdrawn in 1971 and broken up, having led a very useful second life.

In 1963 a unique cooperative membership company was floated by Mr Max Wilson as the Travel Savings Association (TSA). Wilson recognised that a number of passenger liners were being deployed away from their intended services, but that there was an untapped market for relatively cheap 'value for money' sea travel and cruises. Holdings in TSA were wholly owned by Travel Savings Limited, which in turn was owned by British & Commonwealth (parent group of the Union Castle Line), Canadian Pacific and the Max Wilson Organisation. Four ships were chartered into the 'pool'. They were the *Empress of Britain*, to work out of the UK; the *Empress of England*, ostensibly on a five year charter to work out of South Africa; the *Stratheden*; and the *Reina del Mar*, which was then still owned by the Pacific Steam Navigation Company but put under Union Castle management. The *Reina del Mar* was converted with one-class passenger capacity increased by some 300 berths, the installation of a permanent cinema, increased open deck space and additional public rooms. As such she commenced service in June 1964, with her yellow Pacific Steam Navigation Company funnel defaced in blue and the letters TSL enclosed in a circle. The *Stratheden* only did four

cruises before being sold by P&O.

The idea was that passengers paid installments and when they had obtained sufficient credit they could book their cruise. Cruises were run by the *Reina del Mar* and the *Empress of England* in connection with the New York Trade Fair and the Tokyo Olympics in 1964. Although the TSA outwardly looked to be highly successful, Max Wilson pulled out of the scheme in 1965 and it collapsed. The *Empress of England* later went on to the Shaw Savill Line, the *Empress of Britain* to the Greek Line. The *Reina del Mar* became an integral part of the Union Castle Line fleet, being at first under charter from Pacific Steam. Her ownership was later changed to the Royal Mail Line, and in 1973 she was bought by Union Castle. In her cruising role she could accommodate 980 passengers and she retained the magnificent Coral Lounge, possibly the largest room in any liner at that time. One major lesson did come out of the TSA – that rapid turn-arounds between cruises required the development of containerised stores and locked bonded stores for rapid loading and unloading, a

The *Empress of Canada* (1961) commencing her inaugural cruise from Southampton on 21 October 1969.

system since widely adopted by cruise operators and airlines alike.

Under Union Castle colours, the *Reina del Mar* carved herself a valuable niche in the UK and South African cruise markets. In April 1973 a 26-day cruise was advertised at prices from only £265. Her South African cruises to ports in South America were always well patronised and even in August 1974, when it was announced she was to be withdrawn in April the following year, most of her berths had already been sold for the winter season. The reason for her withdrawal was escalating operating costs, particularly the hiked price of fuel oil from 1973 onwards.

Ships of the P&O-Orient fleet were not, for the most part, converted for cruising. Some of the post-war builds such as the *Orcades* and *Orsova* were disposed of as being too old and expensive to adapt for the new role. However, the *Orsova* did carry out some cruising in her final years, and the *Oronsay* carried out a highly successful West Coast America cruise season in 1972. Strangely, the *Orsova* was only sold for demolition in 1974, following a last minute decision to retain the *Canberra*, which had earlier been earmarked for disposal (see Chapter 3). The *Chusan* was used solely as a cruise ship from 1969 but was withdrawn and sold for demolition only four years later. So popular did she become with the so called 'Chusan Club' that special arrangements were made to fly passengers out to Tenerife to return to Southampton on her final inbound sailing from a charter voyage to South Africa. The *Himalaya* was used extensively for cruises and her last UK cruise was a sell-out weekend return from Southampton to Amsterdam, and after one last liner voyage she undertook a final series of cruises out of Australia before she was sold for demolition in 1975. The *Arcadia* took up the role of Australian cruise ship in 1975, and among other alterations for this role she lost her main mast.

In these early days shipboard entertainment became critical during the longer runs at sea. Features included a Ladies' Night, when the ladies chose the wine and asked the men to dance, the Fancy Dress Ball, Country Fair, Music Hall Night and Tropical Island Night. For these, many of the Purser's crew were co-opted to support the Entertainment Officers with the arrangements, but a great time was had by all.

P&O fully recognised the future importance of cruising at an early stage, and in 1973 the

The *Reina del Mar* (1956), resplendent in Union Castle livery, setting off on a cruise from Southampton in May 1968. (See also the photograph on page 26.)

The *Chusan* (1950) at the start of a cruise from Southampton in 1969.

The *Arcadia* (1954) leaving Southampton in June 1968.

appropriate division within P&O was restyled under the brand name P&O Cruises. Both the *Oriana* and the *Canberra* were redesigned as one-class ships with over 1,700 berths each, and deployed on a full-time programme of two- to three-week cruises based at Southampton. The Atlantic Restaurant on the *Canberra* could now seat 704 and she carried a crew of 805. Prices for the *Canberra*'s world cruise in 1976 started at £993 and ranged upwards to £6,450, whereas her final world cruise in 1997 was sold out after three days and prices then ranged from £5,000 to £34,000.

Meanwhile, life on the *Oriana* was not entirely trouble-free. She suffered two engine room fires, one off Fiji and the second only two months later, in August 1970, as she sailed out of Southampton Water at the start of a round the world cruise. With a delayed start of two weeks and at a cost to her owners of £500,000 she finally sailed, her passengers in the meantime entertained as if they had been at sea, coupled with a series of coach trips around southern England. The *Oriana* suffered yet another engine room fire alongside at Southampton in 1981. Throughout her career the *Oriana* steadfastly retained her British crew, whereas the *Canberra* recruited Pakistani seaman and engineers. In fact, it was much to the consternation of the Chief Engineer when the Pakistani engineers had to leave the *Canberra* when she sailed for the Falklands War to spend 94 days at sea with engines that were then 21 years old.

The *Arcadia*, meantime, remained on the Australian cruise programme until 1979 when she was replaced by the *Sea Princess,* formerly the Swedish-America liner *Kungsholm* (see Chapter 10). The *Sea Princess* was transferred to the UK cruise market in 1981 and she in turn was replaced by none other than the *Oriana.* The *Oriana* remained on the Australian cruise service until 1986 when she was sold to Japanese owners for $9.4 million for static use, never again to return to the UK.

The Andes Cruise Club

In 1932 Royal Mail Lines Limited was formed out of the Royal Mail Steam Packet Company, the Nelson Line and the McIver Line. The intermediate service to South America was maintained by the former Nelson Line Monarchs (Chapter 5) and although the main line service was no longer the preserve of the 'Beef Barons' and other millionaires it was still important. The ageing fleet of the main line service was too slow to compete with the French, German and Italian tonnage of the day and consequently an order for a 21-knot single-reduction-geared turbine liner was placed with Harland & Wolff in 1937.

Designed for first and tourist class only, the new *Andes* was intended for off season cruising as a one class ship. Her foremasts were telescopic to allow her to transit the Kiel Canal on her cruising roster. Intended to sail from Southampton on her maiden voyage on 26 September 1939, the exact centenary of the original charter of the Royal Mail Steam Packet Company, she actually left Belfast that same day for the Holy Loch. She was then requisitioned for duties as a troopship. Some of her more expensive fittings were removed at Liverpool and put into store – all were lost in the subsequent bombing raids on the city – and some of the finer panelling was covered over with plywood.

The *Andes* was not released from government service until 1947 when she was returned to her builders for complete refurbishment and partial rebuilding. The first class passenger accommodation was reduced to 324, but tourist class remained at 204. Much of the furniture and fittings had to be rebuilt, but all the accommodation was designed to a very high standard. Her maiden civilian post-war voyage to South America began on 22 January 1948; her first three round trips were fully booked and she

The cruise ship *Andes* (1939) setting out from Southampton in July 1969.

soon became a very popular ship. Her public rooms were spacious and luxurious, although not lavish, and the Promenade Decks were wide.

During the summers between 1956 and 1959 she withdrew from the liner service to run a popular series of cruises to northern capitals, the Mediterranean and even as far as South Africa. In 1959 the new A class ships were coming into service (see Chapter 4) and the *Andes* withdrew from the mail service to become a dedicated cruise ship.

She was sent to Kon Maats de Schelde at Flushing for conversion. One class passenger accommodation was limited to 480, with every cabin fitted with its own bathroom and toilet. The dining saloon was enlarged to provide single sitting service, air conditioning was provided throughout, and the opportunity was taken to upgrade the crew accommodation. A 250-seat cinema was built in one of the former cargo spaces. Four luxury suites were built and the new

'Galleon Grill' was constructed on B Deck. The Lido Deck was extended and a new 'Mermaid Bar' installed. In addition, two 13-metre motor launches were carried, each capable of taking 118 passengers, to act as ship's tenders at cruise destinations. The ship lost her black hull and adopted a very attractive cruising white.

The first cruise under her new guise took place in June 1960. She was soon extremely popular with 60% of her cruise passengers returning for further voyages, usually to the Mediterranean, northern Europe or the Caribbean. This keen following quickly developed into the 'Andes Cruise Club' to assist passengers with their bookings. However, boiler trouble began to cause problems in 1969 and, with a major survey due in 1972, it was decided that the *Andes* could continue no longer. Her last cruise finished on 3 May 1971 and three days later she sailed to the breaker's yard, much to the grief of the Andes Cruise Club.

9. Troopers and School Ships

During the war many ocean liners were used as troop transports and conditions on board were such that forbearance was essential. The three Cunarders *Queen Mary*, *Queen Elizabeth* and *Mauretania*, for example, all carried vast numbers of men to and from the various arenas of war. The two Queens regularly carried up to 15,000 troops each on long voyages. The brand new *Mauretania*, built to carry 1,169 passengers in comfort and style was fitted out to accommodate just 8,000 troops. The passenger cabins were used by officers, female ranks and NCOs. The covered Promenade Decks had hammocks slung from the deck-head beams for 400 men, and sleeping space in the 'tween decks and the garage decks in the holds utilised straw palliasses, although fresh air was at a premium. There was always a shortage of toilets with so many people aboard, and makeshift multiple toilets were arranged along all the outside decks, screened by canvas and draining to overside scuppers.

Peace-time trooping was much less stressful. However, by 1958, the Suez Crisis was over and National Service was no longer obligatory after 1960. In addition, overseas garrisons were being reduced with the contraction of the Empire in favour of the Commonwealth. The new smaller professional army was destined for greater mobility by air (although not in the case of the Falklands War some 20 years later), and this concept was confirmed by a report of the Parliamentary Estimates Committee which declared trooping by air to be the cheaper option. Consequently, in 1962, several troopships became surplus to the requirements of the available government contracts, even though many of these contracts had a good

The British India Line troopship *Dilwara* (1936).

John Shepherd Collection

number of years yet to run.

The troopships were based at Liverpool until 1957, when they were transferred to Southampton. The last remaining troopships were the *Nevasa*, which had been completed for the British India Line in 1956, and the *Oxfordshire* for the Bibby Line in 1957. After only six years of work, both ships were suddenly laid up, the *Nevasa* in the Fal, and the *Oxfordshire* at County Wharf at Falmouth.

Earlier a group of four troopships had been completed in the late 1930s. These were the *Devonshire* for the Bibby Line, the *Ettrick* for the P&O Steam Navigation Company and the *Dunera* and *Dilwara* for the British India Line. They were built as a response to new government trooping regulations and were each just over 11,000 tons gross. They could carry 1,150 troops (who slept in hammocks) plus 104 officers and their families. The ships distinguished themselves at the Salerno landings, were back home for the D-Day operations and were also in the Malaysian landings. However, the third of the group to have been built, the *Ettrick*, was lost off Gibraltar in 1942, having been torpedoed by a U-boat while in convoy.

The *Dilwara* and *Dunera* were the first troopships to be purpose-built for many years. As such, they set new pre-war standards for the carriage of troops and their families. A condition of the design was that they could both operate on conventional British India commercial services if required, but as troop transports with no cargo being carried, 2,500 tons of road metal acted as permanent ballast in numbers 1 to 4 and number 7 holds. For the same reason the passenger accommodation was completed to a very high standard, with the conventional first class music room, smoking room and cafe/lounge on the Promenade Deck. The first class area was in strong contrast to the austerity of the troop decks with their portable tables and hammock hooks. In post-war years the troop decks were partitioned and equipped with bunks. The full complement of these ships was:

Commissioned Officers	104 (First class)
Warrant Officers	100 (Second class)
Troop families	164 (Family accommodation)
Troops	1,154 (Main and Lower Decks)
Crew	209
Total	1,731 men and women

When withdrawn from trooping, the British India Line ships had given well over twenty years service. The *Dunera* was then converted for full time educational cruising, finally emerging for the first time in her long career wearing her owners colours, gone at last was the white hull with broad blue band and the plain buff funnel. The *Dilwara* was sold for further trading to the China Navigation Company in 1960.

The idea behind off-season educational cruises was not new. It had been tried out by the White Star Line and others in the 1930s. The British India Line had also placed the retired troopships *Neuralia* and *Nevasa*, which had originally been built for the UK to Calcutta service in 1912 and 1913 respectively, onto a programme of cheap cruises for parties of schoolboys in 1935. The boys were accommodated on the troop decks with supervisors in the available cabins. With the arrival of the *Dilwara* and *Dunera* in 1936 and 1937, the seasonal cruises were run with the new ships out of the trooping season. They were again targeted at boys who were berthed in the troop quarters with parents, teachers and other adults occupying the passenger cabins.

The troop accommodation was sparse and consisted of hammocks slung at night over daytime mess tables. On the Lower Deck was 'a detention room for disciplinary purposes' and young off-season cruise passengers would have this pointed out to them as warning of misbehaviour! There were extensive medical and hospital areas including a padded cell and a mental ward! The only recreational facilities appear to have been a troops' writing room. The

Seen off Gravesend in August 1965, the *Dunera* (1937) sets off with another shipload of school children.

The schoolship *Devonia* (1939) approaching the Princes Landing Stage at Liverpool in August 1967.

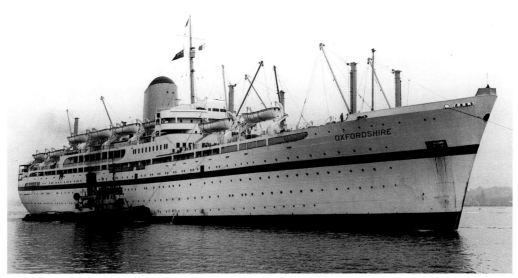

The Bibby Line troopship *Oxfordshire* (1957) at Southampton, with the Red Funnel tug *Clausentum* in attendance. *J & M Clarkson Collection*

elderly *Neuralia* was lost in the war and the *Nevasa* was broken up in 1948.

The conversion of the *Dunera* was the first time that a dedicated school ship was used, complete with classrooms, dormitories and other teaching facilities, as well as a full time Director of Studies. As rebuilt, she could carry 830 school children and adults and now catered for groups of both sexes. The first season of six cruises carried out by the *Dunera* proved highly successful, and as the cruise ship went for her annual overhaul in Genoa in November 1961, her owners announced the purchase of her sister ship *Devonshire* from the Bibby Line.

Conversion was carried out by Barclay, Curle & Company on the Clyde, and under the new name of *Devonia* this ship took up station at Liverpool ready for her inaugural cruise in April 1962. The *Devonia* was also hugely successful in her new role, essentially carrying parties of school children in dormitory accommodation with accompanying teachers in cabin accommodation. School rooms were available

for students to learn about Greek history or Roman architecture as the cruise progressed. There was also excellent accommodation for independent cruise passengers wishing to take advantage of the educational cruise itineraries. Although sisters, the *Devonia* had Sulzer oil engines whereas the *Dunera* was equipped with Doxford machinery.

The success of the school-ship programme eventually released the *Nevasa* from lay up in 1965 for conversion as well. Her near sister the *Oxfordshire* had already left Falmouth on sale to the Fairline Shipping Corporation of Panama, for whom she became the immigrant ship *Fairstar*, and was later used for cruising by P&O-Sitmar. The school ship *Nevasa* was considerably bigger than her new consorts and in addition to the dormitory accommodation (in groups of 12 to 42) for up to 1,090 children, she could carry up to 307 adult passengers. The latter typically comprised about 70 teachers and the rest independent passengers. At the time the company stated that the conversion of the

The *Nevasa* (1956) approaching the Princes Landing Stage at Liverpool in October 1966.

Nevasa represented their faith in what at first was an experiment, but which had subsequently become an established educational service.

The maiden cruise of the *Nevasa* started from Southampton on 28 October carrying parties of children and teachers from Staffordshire. The 13-day voyage included calls at Madeira, Tangier and Lisbon. Her second cruise started at Southampton, but like so many of these cruises ended in the Mediterranean having visited Malta, Piraeus, Izmir and Itea, this time with parties from west Sussex and the borough of Barnet.

With three ships in service between 1965 and 1967, some 37,000 children and 10,000 teachers were catered for annually. The ships became familiar sites in the Mersey, the Clyde, Belfast Lough and Tilbury – wherever it was most convenient for the clientele on offer. In 1967 the *Dunera* was withdrawn from service and sold for demolition, and the *Devonia* followed the following year. There were two reasons for this.

Firstly it would be too costly to bring the ships into line with the new fire regulations brought in by agreement with the United Nations' shipping body, IMCO. Secondly, they were withdrawn in anticipation of the arrival of the newly converted *Uganda* which had just been displaced from the company's London to East Africa service (see Chapter 5) and which was then being refitted as an educational cruise ship at the Howaldtswerke shipyard in Hamburg.

The *Uganda* was considerably altered when she emerged from the shipyard. A great effort had been made to update the ship as well as remodel her accommodation for the new role. She now had a mainmast only and a totally new bridge structure. Dormitory accommodation was available for about 900 children, while teachers were accommodated in three-berth cabins with a number of additional cabins available for independent passengers. While at sea, the school day was broken up into five 45-minute periods. These were devoted to

'Assembly Hall', where members of the ship's educational staff would lecture the students on some aspect of the next port of call, 'Deck Games', 'Private Study' or 'Classrooms'. With perhaps three teachers supervising about 45 children each, incidents were inevitable. One teacher, Mr R Baker with a party of children from Southampton, commented on the relief on having put his children to bed, only to hear over the 'Tannoy' that the ship had been steaming back along her own wake for the past two hours searching for a missing boy. The report continues (as first published in *Sea Breezes*, November 1969):

> The atmosphere for about a quarter of an hour that this crisis lasted can be imagined. It was relieved, however, by the discovery of the missing youth in a life-boat. If, and how he was punished I do not know, but the feeling among one or two people aboard can, I think, be imagined . . . As the *Uganda* continued on to Tenerife and Madeira, the daily routines were slightly altered to allow for several interesting variations. The first of these were the bridge and engine room visits which were usually taken by junior officers and cadets. These men gave very full explanations to the parties and the boys were of course very interested, but I suspected that some of it was rather above the girls and that they became more interested in the young officers rather than in their duties. The other events were the ship's concert and the fancy dress ball...

An article in the *Daily Mail* in May 1969 by the Director of Studies, Mr Michael Reeves, described "Passion patrols laid on by the ship's crew . . . [which] kept an eye on gymslip sweethearts". Problems ashore included the time when an Arab businessman wanted to buy three attractive sixth form girls for his harem! In short, a ship-load of adolescents of both sexes, along with independently booked adult passengers could be a sensitive mix, and there needed to be overall acceptance that discipline had to be firm, though short of draconian. One other problem arose in October 1969 when the *Uganda*, complete with 900 passengers, apparently strayed into a target practice area and was fired on by a Spanish shore battery!

The two school-ships continued in service until 'unprecedented increases in operating costs' forced the withdrawal of the *Nevasa* from the school-ship programme at the end of 1974. At that time there had been a rapid fourfold increase in fuel oil costs and crew, maintenance and support services had risen in cost at a faster rate than it was feasible to increase passenger fares, particularly for student passengers, in the prevailing economic climate. A statement from Mr John Sharpe, P&O's Educational Cruise manager read:

> Educational cruising has been a marginal operation for some time due to cost escalation which has hit the *Nevasa* harder than the *Uganda* due to higher manning and fuel consumption costs. Further costs simply could not be absorbed without jeopardising the whole educational cruising programme, and for this reason we have, after very careful study, reluctantly decided to withdraw the *Nevasa* from service.

She lay at Malta for over a year before proceeding to Taiwan for demolition.

The *Uganda* continued the programme alone. In 1976 she visited 60 different ports on 27 cruises, 13 of which were winter fly-cruises to the eastern Mediterranean. By the early 1980s the last remaining school ship was finding it difficult to attract the numbers that been forthcoming earlier. Hit by worldwide inflation, the fares for a two week voyage were beyond many parents' means, even though the demand from adult passengers remained strong.

The *Uganda* finished her career as a school ship without warning in 1982, when called up to serve as a hospital ship in the Falklands War. On this occasion the children were ordered ashore at Naples and flown home, their holiday

The *Uganda* (1952) coming into Southampton at the end of a cruise in February 1968.

peremptorily cut short. Conversion for use as a hospital ship included the fitting of a satellite communication system, a helicopter pad, a reverse osmosis plant for fresh water plus repainting in the colours of the International Red Cross. All this took just 65 hours. She carried 32 medical officers and 140 medical ratings, and in her 113 days as a hospital ship a total of 750 patients received treatment, 159 of them within an intensive four hour period following the bombing of the *Sir Galahad*. The *Uganda* was later used as a transport between Ascension and the Falklands, and when this contract ended in 1985 she sailed to Falmouth 'for orders'.

P&O stated that renovations, including removal of the helicopter landing pad would not be cost effective, and she was laid up awaiting sale for demolition. In due course she was sold, but foundered en route to the breaker's yard before the cutting torches could get to her.

For a short while after the *Uganda* was taken off the school-ship programme an alternative service was provided by Sussex-based 'Schools Abroad'. They initially used the former Irish Sea ferry *Duke of Argyll*, which had been converted for cruising under the Cypriot flag as the *Neptunia*, but later a variety of Greek ships were chartered for short periods.

10. The Cruising Lifeline

Realisation that cruising was the way forward dawned in the early 1970s when both Cunard and P&O were bent on building dedicated cruise ships. Strangely, they were all ordered by foreign companies and acquired during construction. The first was the unoriginally named *Cunard Adventurer*, ordered in the first instance by Overseas National Airways, an American airline, but completed in collaboration with the Cunard Steamship Company under the new ownership of Cunard-ONA Limited. The second, for P&O, was the *Spirit of London*, ordered originally as one of a pair by Lauritz Kloster.

The *Cunard Adventurer* had a passenger capacity of 806 in 31 outside 'de luxe' double cabins, 178 outside doubles, 104 inside doubles and four single cabins. Her gross tonnage was only 14,151. Seven out of the ten decks were for passenger use. There was a swimming pool, a Lido Deck, restaurant, lounge, night club (the 329 Club, named after the builders yard number for the ship), six bars, a hairdressing salon, sauna and massage rooms, shops, cinema and the Sky Room bar with panoramic views and situated above the wheelhouse. She was equipped with four Stork-Werkspoor oil engines and could maintain a service speed of 21 knots. Her maiden cruise – to the Caribbean – took place in November 1971; it was an inauspicious start as she broke down in the Bay of Biscay, and had to limp into Lisbon to await a replacement housing for the starboard propeller shaft to be flown out. A second ship, the *Cunard Ambassador,* was completed in 1972.

The new P&O ship was heralded by Mr Jim Davis, a company director:

The USA is the largest potential market for cruising in the world, and in our new cruise ship we are certain that we can offer discriminating American passengers a fine cruising ship. The *Spirit of London* is the first of our second tier passenger fleet of small purpose-built cruise ships, designed to retain P&O's world leadership in cruising right through the 1980s.

Intended for short duration cruises in the Caribbean, the American market was developed alongside the European fly-cruise. The ship also had oil engines, twin Fiat units, which gave her a speed of 20 knots. A crew of 334 catered for 730 passengers in 409 cabins, all of which were equipped with toilets, baths or showers, a radio and telephone. The emphasis was very much on entertainment and accommodation of first-class hotel standard. The new ship sailed from Southampton in November 1972 on a positioning cruise to the Caribbean.

Just before the *Spirit of London* was built, a slightly larger ship, the *Sea Venture* was being completed for Norwegian Cruiseships A/S of Oslo. Designed for the New York to Caribbean cruise market she had 324 cabins of which 47 were de-luxe, giving her a passenger capacity of 749. She too was equipped with Fiat oil engines and could maintain a service speed of 21 knots. On completion, she carried a crew of 301, of which 265 were employed on the hotel side of the ship. The Lounge Deck contained two large lounges, a multi-purpose theatre, four dance floors and three bars. There were two heated swimming pools, one aft on the Lounge Deck, the other on the Sun Deck. A second ship, the *Island Venture* was commissioned in 1972.

Two years later P&O acquired the Canadian company Princess Cruises. This company had been using a variety of chartered tonnage for cruises to the Caribbean, Mexico and, in summer, to Alaska. It was logical that P&O should transfer the *Spirit of London* to their new venture, and in October 1974 she was renamed *Sun Princess*. In addition, a deal was struck to

The *Island Princess* (1972) leaving Southampton in August 1996.

The *Pacific Princess* (1971) setting off from the Tilbury Landing Stage in July 1987.

The Lido Buffet aboard the *Pacific Princess* (1971). *Princess Cruises*

acquire the two new Norwegian liners, and in April 1975 the *Sea Venture* raised the Red Ensign as the *Pacific Princess* and the *Island Venture* as the *Island Princess*.

Typical Princess Cruises destinations in the mid 1970s were as follows:

Island Princess – Caribbean cruise from Los Angeles to Acapulco, Panama, Aruba, Caracas, Port of Spain, St Thomas, Freeport, and Port Everglades.

Pacific Princess – Alaskan cruise from Los Angeles to San Francisco, Victoria, Prince Rupert, Sitka, Glacier Bay, Skagway, Juneau, Vancouver and return direct.

Sun Princess – Mexican cruise from Los Angeles to Puerto Vallarta, Manzanillo, Acapulco, Mazatlan and Cabo San Lucas and return to Los Angeles.

The two Cunarders also spent much of their time cruising in the Caribbean. The *Cunard Adventurer* suffered an engine room fire in July 1974, but was soon repaired. However, in September 1974, an even worse engine room fire occurred, this time on the *Cunard Ambassador* while she was on an empty positioning run between Port Everglades and New Orleans. Some 190 of the crew of 240 were taken off by a US naval tanker but, as the emergency power failed, the cruise ship was abandoned. Later towed to an anchorage off Key West, she was declared beyond repair and was sold for further use after conversion into a livestock carrier. Ironically a second engine room fire in 1984 sent her to the scrap yard. The *Cunard Adventurer* only remained in the Cunard fleet until 1976 when she was displaced by new building. She remains in service under the Greek flag as the *Triton*.

The *Cunard Countess* (1976) backing up to the quay at Road Town, British Virgin Islands.

The new ships were the *Cunard Countess* and *Cunard Princess*, the latter launched as the *Cunard Conquest*. The ships were based at San Juan in Puerto Rico. These were larger ships than the first pair and had a gross tonnage of 17,586. The *Cunard Countess* left Burmeister & Wain's yard at Copenhagen after her launch in September 1974 for fitting out in Italy, arriving on station at San Juan in August 1976. Her younger sister joined her the following year. They had eight passenger decks and had berths for 750 passengers in 373 cabins. Public rooms included a panoramic observation lounge, a night club/cinema, a casino and a 371 seater restaurant. They were equipped with the customary shop and hairdressing salon, an activities room which doubled as a conference room, a children's room which could also be used as a private dining room, and there were seven bars. With the funnel placed well aft, there were large open deck areas as well as a heated swimming pool just forward of the funnel. The

ships settled into the weekly pattern of fly cruises drawing on both the UK and US markets.

Initially very profitable ships, they became more expensive to operate throughout the 1970s. In October 1980 Cunard announced the transfer of the two ships to the Bahamian flag and the replacement of many of the British crew members with a locally recruited crew. On hearing this news, the *Cunard Countess* immediately became strikebound on her weekly visit to Bridgetown in Barbados. However, the transfer was completed in October 1980 for the *Cunard Princess* only, and as consolation the *Cunard Countess* was allowed to retain her British port of registry.

Relief to her owners finally came as a result of the Falklands War when the *Cunard Countess* was chartered to maintain the 6,500 km ferry between the Falklands and Ascension Island, which was the strategic limit of air troop transport en route to the 'deep south'. On return to civilian duties the two ships again maintained their San Juan station but also undertook a new programme of Mediterranean-based cruises. In December 1990 the *Cunard Princess* was chartered to the US government for nine months for use as a 'rest and recuperation' centre for American military personnel then stationed in the Middle East during the Gulf War. The American soldiers came aboard for their cruise to nowhere every three days in batches of 900. They were treated to every amenity on the ship, save for the casino, and all was found for them save for their bar bills, even civilian clothes were provided if necessary. The ships were sold in 1995 and 1996 respectively, the *Cunard Princess* for further service in the Mediterranean and the *Cunard Countess* for use out of Singapore as the *Awani Dream II*. In 1997 she became the *Olympic Countess* based in the Mediterranean, and is little altered from her days as a Cunard ship.

The *Queen Elizabeth 2* took on an increasing role as a cruise ship as time went on. As the situation deteriorated over the sovereignty of the Falkland Islands, Cunard took out special insurance against her being called up for service. But in May 1982, within only one week of agreeing the policy, she was requisitioned at Southampton to carry 3,500 troops, the Fifth Infantry Brigade, to join the main task force. She was converted into a troopship in only eight days: helicopter decks were fitted, soft furniture and grand pianos were put in store, and carpets were covered. Provisions were taken aboard for 90 days. She sailed to South Georgia without escort using fog and icebergs for cover. Captain Peter Jackson reported:

> We had no escort. No ship was fast enough to keep up with us. We had no air cover. Once we got into the hostile area we fitted up a gun emplacement on each wing of the bridge with two Browning automatics. There was no real defence. Of course we did have more than 3,000 rifles on board and they could have given an aircraft some trouble.

The *Queen Elizabeth 2* (1968) in Southampton Water in the summer of 1991.

The *Queen Elizabeth 2* returned from South Georgia directly to the UK ahead of most of the rest of the fleet of transports. She returned with the survivors from the warships HMS *Coventry*, HMS *Antelope* and HMS *Ardent* as well as the container ship *Atlantic Conveyor*, all of which had been lost to enemy missile attacks. The *Queen Elizabeth 2* subsequently underwent a £10 million refit, emerging with a new health club called the Golden Door, a pale grey hull and, at last, the Cunard funnel colours instead of the all white funnel she had worn before. She sailed for New York in August 1983 and prices for the single trip ranged up to £2,500. Prices have increased subsequently, but starting at £14,250 for the 1996 world cruise works out at only 1.8 pence per kilometre as against the traditional cruise rate in the depressed 1930s of 1.3 pence per kilometre.

In 1987 the *Queen Elizabeth 2* finally lost her turbine engines in favour of a new set of diesel electric machinery, and this was claimed at the time to offer a 50% cut in fuel consumption. Outwardly the only change was a slightly enlarged funnel top to accommodate the exhaust pipes from the nine diesel units. At the same time that this work was carried out, changes were also made to public rooms, and the ship's main restaurant became the Mauretania Room.

The *Canberra* was also requisitioned for war service, and stories of the 'Great White Whale' in 'bomb alley' have become legend. The ship was refuelled several times at sea on the passage south, and eventually returned from war duties to Southampton in July 1982. The other requisitioned liner was the *Uganda* which was dispatched in mid-cruise to Gibraltar for conversion to a hospital ship. Although the *Canberra* returned to a long and successful civilian life afterwards, the *Uganda* was deemed unworthy of renovation and was eventually sold (see Chapter 9).

The *Sea Princess* (1966) leaving Southampton on a cruise in July 1985.

In 1978 P&O bought the *Sea Princess* on the second hand market in order to develop the company's role in the cruise market. This ship had been built by John Brown & Company on the Clyde for the Swedish-America Line as the *Kungsholm* twelve years previously in 1966. She had been designed as a dual role North Atlantic liner and New York-based cruise ship, but was sold for use under the Bermudan and later the Liberian flags. On purchase by P&O she was sent to the Bremer Vulkan shipyard in Bremen for an extensive refit. Outwardly her forward funnel and mainmast were removed and the remaining aft funnel extended. Internally little changed; even the paintings on the bulkheads remained as before. However, 86 new cabins were installed so that 840 passengers could be accommodated in 400 cabins. A swimming pool was built alongside the new Carousel Lounge on the Promenade Deck. Otherwise her main public rooms, including the Princess Theatre, Pacific Lounge and Tasman Restaurant remained unchanged, other than in name.

The *Sea Princess* arrived at Sydney, via Hong Kong, in March 1979 ready to take over the Australian cruise programme from the *Arcadia*. The new ship brought a level of luxury hitherto unseen in the Antipodes, and this was much publicised by her owners. She then carried a British crew, the officers rostered for four months duty with two months off, whereas other ranks did four months on against one month leave. In addition there were Pakistani seamen and engine room artificers as well as Goanese dining room stewards and the obligatory Chinese laundry.

Most cabins had a writing desk and a sitting room area curtained off from the 'bedroom'. The luxury ship did not stay long in Australian waters and was transferred to the premier cruise grounds of the Mediterranean in 1981. The new accent was on elegance and luxury, leaving the old *Oriana* to continue the Australian cruise programme – P&O were at pains to point out that the decision to withdraw the *Sea Princess* did not belittle the qualities of the old *Oriana*!

11. Evolution of the Cruise Ship

The cruise ship has become quite a different breed from the passenger liner. The cruise ship carries no cargo and it tends to make a landfall in the early morning for passengers to run ashore ready for an evening departure and another landfall the next morning. This daily routine is based on the premise that two days and more at sea is too long for a cruise ship to entertain its passengers without a port of call. The cruise ship has evolved in a number of other directions. Economy of scale, whereby the more passengers carried per ton of fuel oil, per crew member, per unit capital depreciation, mean that new builds have inevitably got larger. The ships have also become broader in the beam to retain the essential shallow draught for entry to many of the more popular cruise destinations. Passenger cabins have developed in sophistication, many now have their own private veranda and all but the cheapest cabins have access to daylight in some form or another. Other developments include the technical advances of using lower grade fuel oil, energy conservation and preheating of fuel, as well as thrust units and pod-mounted propellers with overall enhanced manoeuvrability developed originally for the benefit of cross-channel ferries.

Princess Cruises, based in Los Angeles, underwent major expansion with the might of P&O behind it. In 1988 Princess Cruises took over Sitmar Cruises and with it three new buildings including the *Sitmar Fairmajesty*, which was delivered by her builders at St Nazaire in the spring of 1989 as the *Star Princess*. Like so many of the modern cruise ships, she has a central feature around a sweeping circular staircase that dominates the three deck Plaza. The lower level contains the

The *Arcadia* (1989) seen at Southampton at the start of a summer season cruise.

main lobby, reception area and a patisserie. The upper levels offer the Emerald and Promenade Decks, the Galleria shopping arcade and wine bar. Other ships to come under the Princess banner from Sitmar were the *Fairsea* and *Fairwind*, which were originally the Cunard Line's *Carinthia* and *Sylvania* (see Chapter 2), and the former Bibby Line troopship *Oxfordshire* (see Chapter 9) which had since become the *Fairstar*.

The *Star Princess* has 735 twin berth cabins plus 14 suites and 36 mini suites with outdoor terraces. Of the cabins, 510 have outside picture windows, 165 are inside cabins and ten are wheelchair accessible. The ship has a crew of 563. Although the *Star Princess* has a draught of 7.7 m, her registered gross tonnage is a massive 62,500. Normal operational speed is 19.5 knots, but the diesel electric propulsion machinery can maintain up to 22.5 knots if required. Otherwise a highly successful ship, in 1995 she struck Poundstone Rock near Juneau in Alaska, terminating a cruise prematurely with two long gashes down her starboard side.

Typical of modern design is her two-level Starlight Showlounge which can seat 708 passengers. The dining room, the Fountain Court, seats 801 on multi-levels and makes plentiful use of the sea views through large windows. Formerly registered in Liberia, the ship was transferred in 1997 to the P&O Cruises UK-based fleet as a direct replacement for the *Canberra*, was renamed *Arcadia*, and re-registered in London. The elderly, if not venerable, *Canberra* was then sold for demolition, the shipbreakers complaining bitterly that they had lost money on the deal as the old ship was more strongly built than they had anticipated! The *Arcadia* received many artifacts and adornments from the *Canberra* when she took up service from the UK. She joined the brand new *Oriana*, and the *Sea Princess* (see Chapter 10), which was renamed *Victoria* to bring her into line with current nomenclature and to release her name back to Princess Cruises.

The former *Sea Princess* (1966) sporting the new name of *Victoria* on a wet day at Southampton in 1998.

On an evening departure from Southampton, the *Oriana* (1995) is seen in her second year of service.

The *Oriana* had been delivered from the German Papenburg yard of JL Meyer GmbH in time for her official naming by the Queen on 6 March 1995 at Southampton. The ship has some impressive statistics, not least that with a gross tonnage of 69,153 her draught is only 7.9 m. Two pairs of medium speed 'father and son' oil engines (nine and six cylinders respectively) give her a relatively fast design speed of 24 knots. The *Oriana* is highly manoeuvrable with twin rudders, three bow thruster units and one thruster unit at the stern.

There are ten passenger decks; the Promenade Deck features the main entertainment areas with spacious teak decked margins. At the forward end, the Theatre Royal seats up to 650, complete with an orchestra pit and a revolving stage. Adjacent is the four-deck high marble-clad atrium, complete with full height waterfall. Other public rooms include the oak panelled Andersons lounge bar; a casino; the Lord's Tavern pub; Harlequin's, which is a multi-purpose dance/disco/night club area; and the Pacific Lounge.

'D' Deck, which is above the main Promenade Deck, houses children's facilities, a 200 seat cinema, quiet lounge and library. With the engines set three-quarters aft, the deck area is very spacious. There are two swimming pools, one 14 m long, and the Oasis health spa and Conservatory Cafe. The main restaurants are down below on 'E' Deck with the Peninsular Restaurant amidships and the Oriental Restaurant aft, the latter complete with a 17 m-long mural of the 'Story of Odysseus'. There are 3,000 paintings on board, including two in each cabin, and a magnificent embroidery, 'Glimpses of India', which adorns the Curzon Room.

The *Oriana* has eight suites, 16 de luxe staterooms and 94 other staterooms on 'B' Deck, plus 590 two bed cabins (some with additional Pullman berths) on Decks 'A' to 'F'. There is also a selection of one-, three- and some four-berth cabins. All are well appointed and self contained. Her maiden voyage took her

(Continued on page 119)

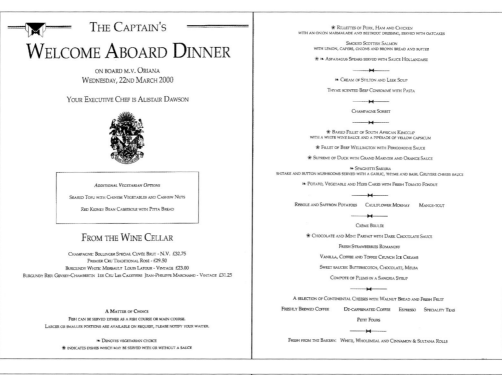

THE CAPTAIN'S
WELCOME ABOARD DINNER

ON BOARD M.V. ORIANA
WEDNESDAY, 22ND MARCH 2000

YOUR EXECUTIVE CHEF IS ALISTAIR DAWSON

Additional Vegetarian Options

SEARED TOFU WITH CHINESE VEGETABLES AND CASHEW NUTS

RED KIDNEY BEAN CASSEROLE WITH PITTA BREAD

FROM THE WINE CELLAR

CHAMPAGNE: BOLLINGER SPECIAL CUVÉE BRUT - N.V. £32.75
PREMIER CRU TRADITIONAL ROSÉ - £29.50
BURGUNDY WHITE: MEURSAULT LOUIS LATOUR - VINTAGE £23.00
BURGUNDY RED: GEVREY-CHAMBERTIN 1ER CRU LES CAZETIERS JEAN-PHILIPPE MARCHAND - VINTAGE £31.25

A MATTER OF CHOICE

FISH CAN BE SERVED EITHER AS A FISH COURSE OR MAIN COURSE.
LARGER OR SMALLER PORTIONS ARE AVAILABLE ON REQUEST, PLEASE NOTIFY YOUR WAITER.

🍃 DENOTES VEGETARIAN CHOICE
✱ INDICATES DISHES WHICH MAY BE SERVED WITH OR WITHOUT A SAUCE

✱ RILLETTES OF PORK, HAM AND CHICKEN
WITH AN ONION MARMALADE AND BEETROOT DRESSING, SERVED WITH OATCAKES

SMOKED SCOTTISH SALMON
WITH LEMON, CAPERS, ONIONS AND BROWN BREAD AND BUTTER

✱ 🍃 ASPARAGUS SPEARS SERVED WITH SAUCE HOLLANDAISE

🍃 CREAM OF STILTON AND LEEK SOUP

THYME SCENTED BEEF CONSOMMÉ WITH PASTA

CHAMPAGNE SORBET

✱ BAKED FILLET OF SOUTH AFRICAN KINGCLIP
WITH A WHITE WINE SAUCE AND A PIPÉRADE OF YELLOW CAPSICUM

✱ FILLET OF BEEF WELLINGTON WITH PERIGORDINE SAUCE

✱ SUPREME OF DUCK WITH GRAND MARNIER AND ORANGE SAUCE

🍃 SPAGHETTI SAKURA
SHITAKE AND BUTTON MUSHROOMS SERVED WITH A GARLIC, THYME AND BASIL GRUYÈRE CHEESE SAUCE

🍃 POTATO, VEGETABLE AND HERB CAKES WITH FRESH TOMATO FONDUE

RISSOLE AND SAFFRON POTATOES   CAULIFLOWER MORNAY   MANGE-TOUT

CRÈME BRÛLÉE

✱ CHOCOLATE AND MINT PARFAIT WITH DARK CHOCOLATE SAUCE

FRESH STRAWBERRIES ROMANOFF

VANILLA, COFFEE AND TOFFEE CRUNCH ICE CREAMS

SWEET SAUCES: BUTTERSCOTCH, CHOCOLATE, MELBA

COMPOTE OF PLUMS IN A SANGRIA SYRUP

A SELECTION OF CONTINENTAL CHEESES WITH WALNUT BREAD AND FRESH FRUIT

FRESHLY BREWED COFFEE   DE-CAFFEINATED COFFEE   ESPRESSO   SPECIALITY TEAS

PETIT FOURS

FRESH FROM THE BAKERY: WHITE, WHOLEMEAL AND CINNAMON & SULTANA ROLLS

ORIANA

Saturday, 25th March 2000

Your Executive Chef is Alistair Dawson

From the Wine Cellar

Champagne:
Moet & Chandon Brut Impérial - Vintage £34.50

Sparkling Champagne:
Cremant Da Loire - £17.50

Australian White:
Chardonnay Rosemount Estate - Vintage £12.35

New Zealand Red:
Cabernet Merlot Vidal Estate - Vintage £14.50

Additional Vegetarian Options

Macaroni Cheese with Oyster Mushrooms

🍃 Denotes vegetarian choice
✱ indicates dishes which may be served with or without a sauce

---

A matter of choice
Fish can be served either as a fish course or main course
Small or large portions are available on request, please notify your Waiter

---

✱ 🍃 Warm Salad of Marinated Goat Cheese
with apples, walnuts and crème fraîche

Mushroom Ravioli
with a herb and tomato sauce

✱ Prawn Cocktail in a light Natural Yoghurt and Tomato Sauce

❖

Beef and Vegetable Broth

Game Consommé with Redcurrant Jelly and Venison Medallions

❖

✱ Baked Fillet of South African Musselcracker with White Wine, Tomatoes and Brunoise of Vegetables

✱ Roast Turkey with Cocktail Sausage, Chestnut Stuffing with Cranberry Sauce

Sauté of Fillet Beef Stroganoff
*strips of tender fillet beef with onions and sliced mushroom in a sherry cream sauce with paprika,
served with saffron rice*

✱ Medallions of Pork with crisp Sage and toasted Almonds
served with a sauce charcutiere

🍃 Vegetarian Chilli with Pitta Bread

Carrots Vichy   Brussels Sprouts   Duchesse & Fondant Potatoes

Black Forest Pudding with Custard Sauce
Poire Belle Héléne
✱ Petit Choux Swan Chantilly with Apricot Sauce
Vanilla, Mint Chocolate Chip and Toffee Ice Creams
Sweet Sauces: Butterscotch Chocolate Melba
Compote of Rhubarb in Ginger Wine
Lemon Sorbet

❖

A selection of British and Continental Cheeses with Biscuits

Fresh Fruit

❖

Freshly Brewed Coffee   De-Caffeinated   Espresso   Cappuccino   Speciality Teas
Macaroons

Fresh from the Bakery
White, Wholemeal, Malted Wheat and Garlic Rolls

D4

Menus from a cruise by the *Oriana* in March 2000.

ORIANA TODAY

8.30PM & 10.30PM
THEATRE ROYAL

WITH THE VOCAL TALENT OF
JACQUI SCOTT

THE GREAT VOICE AND PERSONALITY OF
PAUL EMMANUEL

AND THE COMEDY OF
DON REID

FEATURING **THE STADIUM THEATRE COMPANY**
MUSICAL ACCOMPANIMENT BY **THE ROGER CARR ORCHESTRA**

8.30pm & 10.30pm - *Curzon Room*

The Armadillo String Quartet of Canada
Presents "Bach to the Beatles"

The Armadillo String Quartet presents a concert of music through the ages.
Their electric style takes you on a musical journey from...
"Bach to the Beatles."

NOON
PACIFIC LOUNGE

CRUISE DIRECTOR'S INTRODUCTIONS

CRUISE ALONG TO HEAR *NIGEL TRAVIS*, CRUISE DIRECTOR
INTRODUCE HIS TEAM OF *ENTERTAINMENT OFFICERS*.

CAPTAIN'S RECEPTION PARTIES

1st sitting at 6.00pm
2nd sitting at 8.00pm

Passengers who dine in the
Peninsular Restaurant
are invited to the Crow's Nest
(Deck 13)

Passengers who dine in the
Oriental Restaurant
are invited to the Pacific Lounge
(Deck 7)

Photographers will be taking
pictures outside the Pacific Lounge
from 30 minutes before the
commencement of each party.

DRESS FOR TODAY

Formal: Dinner jacket or dark suit and tie for gentlemen; long or short evening wear for ladies.

SHIP'S CLOCKS

Ship's clocks will be put back one hour at 2.00am tomorrow (Wednesday).

SUNRISE & SUNSET

Sunrise: 7.17am   Sunset: 7.38pm

The cover of the onboard publication *Oriana Today.*

Luggage label from the *Oriana*'s cruise in March 2000.

(Continued from page 116)
passengers to the Atlantic Isles for 12 nights, with fares starting at £1,199.

When new, *Star Princess* (later the *Arcadia*) had joined the Princess fleet in 1989. Until then it had been largely an all UK registered fleet: the *Royal Princess*, *Sea Princess*, which had been transferred from P&O Cruises in 1985, *Sun Princess* (ex-*Spirit of London*) and the sisters *Pacific Princess* and *Island Princess* (see Chapter 10). The *Royal Princess* had been built at the Wartsila Shipyard at Helsinki and commenced her maiden voyage from Southampton in November 1984. It was about this time that Trafalgar House, which had bought Cunard in 1971, was making overtures to P&O, having acquired 5% of P&O's shares by 1983. A

slanging match ensued between the two companies with P&O describing Cunard as 'messing about in boats'. The arrival of the new ship was an excellent means of putting the failed hostile bid into the past. The *Royal Princess* cost $150 million and featured the new concept of 'all outside' cabin accommodation for 1,200 passengers. Of these cabins, 152 of the staterooms and the suites on Decks 7 and 8 have their own balconies.

The overall theme of the ship is of that of an international top calibre hotel. With eight passenger decks, the main public rooms are on Deck 3, the Riviera Deck, and Deck 2, the Plaza Deck. The central and impressive Plaza itself is two decks high, and the adjacent Continental dining room seats 616 on two levels, while the International Lounge on the Riviera Deck seats 612 for entertainment of a lavish style, akin more to Broadway than the West End. The Sun and Lido Decks offer the expected array of swimming pools, lounges and cafes. There is also a nightclub, a casino and health club. At Deck 4 level a promenade area completely encircles the whole ship. The *Royal Princess* has a gross tonnage of 44,348 and has a service speed of 22 knots. She requires a crew of 500.

The *Sun Princess* (formerly the *Spirit of London*) left the fleet in 1988 for further service under the Bahamian flag. Notwithstanding, the fleet stood at 16 ships by 1994, carrying 430,000 cruise passengers to 250 ports in 100 different countries. Only one of the more recently acquired ships was then registered in London. The *Sky Princess*, which was completed in 1984 as the *Fairsky* for the Sitmar Line, was that company's flagship when Princess Cruises acquired them in 1988. The ship has never featured in either UK or Mediterranean-based cruising although she proudly carried her port of registry as London, until transferred temporarily to Liberian registry in 1999. Much of her time has been spent on Alaskan cruises, although she has now become the regular Far Eastern cruise ship under the name *Pacific Sky*.

The *Royal Princess* (1984) leaving Tilbury to view the Thames Barrage at the start of a cruise in June 1990.

The *Sun Princess* (1995) poses for the camera with her new Red Ensign in Alaska.   *Princess Cruises*

The lavish space-age casino aboard the *Sun Princess* (1995) is a far cry from the traditional passenger liner.

Princess Cruises

The *Sky Princess* (1984) was British registered on acquisition from Sitmar Cruises in 1988. She was renamed *Pacific Sky* on transfer to P&O Cruises Australia in Autumn 2000.   *Princess Cruises*

She claims the distinction of being the very last British-flagged steam turbine passenger ship.

Displaced by the larger new tonnage, the elderly *Island Princess* also left the fleet, joining the South Korean Hyundai Group as the *Hyundai Pungak-Ho* in the summer of 1999. This rapid sale necessitated offering passengers alternative cruises on the *Pacific Princess* which was then offering a similar itinerary. The *Pacific Princess* continues for the moment, under the marketing strategy that she is small and friendly.

Purchase of the Italian Sitmar Line came about due to that company's far-sighted ordering of new tonnage. Princess Cruises

desperately needed to expand, and the acquisition of the existing Sitmar fleet, and more importantly its new buildings, allowed the required expansion of Princess Cruises. As a consequence, much of the fleet retained Italian crews and Italian registry, although some of the fleet was registered in Liberia in the mid-1990s in order to attract tax benefits.

The latest unit to join the Princess Cruises fleet is the *Ocean Princess* (see Table 3). She was delivered by Fincantieri Catieri Navali Italiani for a price believed to be greater than $300

(Continued on page 124)

The latest addition to the fleet, the *Ocean Princess* (2000), was transferred from Liberian registry to that of London before her maiden voyage.   *Princess Cruises*

One of the five ships to be transferred by Princess Cruises to British registry in 2000 was the *Sea Princess* (1998), seen arriving at Fort Lauderdale, Florida.   *Princess Cruises*

Also transferred to the Red Ensign was the *Regal Princess* (1991), a ship distinguished by a most unimaginative funnel arrangement. *Princess Cruises*

An outside double cabin with private veranda aboard the *Regal Princess* (1991). *Princess Cruises*

The diminutive *Hebridean Princess* (1964) returning to Oban on her weekly cruise roster during summer 1998.

(Continued from page 121)
million in February 2000. Prior to her maiden voyage she was transferred to UK registry, and this reflagging was followed shortly afterwards by the previously Liberian registered *Sun Princess* and *Sea Princess*. By May the *Dawn Princess* and *Regal Princess* were also under the Red Ensign.

Transfer of these large and modern cruise ships to the UK registry reflected both the high standards maintained by Princess Cruises and the demerger of parent Group P&O to create the new UK-based parent company of P&O Cruises.

The smallest of the British cruise ships in recent years has been the little *Hebredian Princess*. She is equipped to transport 49 passengers in de luxe country hotel style accommodation around the Western Isles of Scotland, and to Scandinavian and Irish Sea destinations. She was built in 1964 as a side-loading vehicle and passenger ferry for the Scottish operator Caledonian MacBrayne, in which guise she was licensed to carry 600 passengers. Hebridean Island Cruises bought the ferry in 1989 and completely rebuilt her internally with considerable external modification as well. She is extremely well patronised with a very high repeat booking clientele. Ownership of the company changed hands in 1999 but the cruise service remains unchanged. She will be joined in 2001 by a second ship, the *Hebridean Spirit*, which will be aimed at small ship clintele looking at up-market cruising, but this time to international destinations.

The latest new building for the P&O fleet is the *Aurora*, completed in 2000 as a development of the *Oriana* design, for use in the UK cruise market. The ship is some 76,000 tons gross, with a relatively shallow draught of only 7.9 m, and has a service speed of 24 knots. The new *Aurora* features four decks of cabins with private deck space, and there is a swimming pool with a

The brand new *Aurora* (2000) arriving at Southampton from her builders on 16 April 2000.   *Stephanie Robins*

retractable megadrome roof. In all, 1,975 passengers can be accommodated in 934 cabins. P&O Cruises have two more new buildings scheduled for P&O and five more for Princess Cruises for delivery by 2004.

From time to time, certain cruise ships have adopted UK registry for brief periods. The Lowline-operated turbine steamer *Edinburgh Castle* was one such ship, marketed in the UK by Direct Cruises in the late 1990s. She was formerly the *Eugenio Costa*. Although the idea of low cost cruising booked directly with the operator was attractive, the ship, which also undertook gambling cruises out of New York, was plagued with mechanical and operational problems and her owners soon went out of business. The former *Empress of Canada* (see Chapter 2), no longer UK registered and now trading as the *Apollon*, has, however, been used to better effect in this same trade. Also in the 1990s the two small explorer-type cruise ships

Sea Goddess I and *Sea Goddess II* were registered in the Isle of Man for Cunard, before transferring to Norwegian registration as part of the Seabourn arm of Cunard under the names *Seabourn Goddess I* and *Seabourn Goddess II* in 1999.

The latest addition to the Cunard Line is the recently refurbished *Caronia* (formerly the *Vistafjord*), which was re-registered at the end of 1999 at Southampton for use in the UK cruise market. Built by Swan Hunter Shipbuilders Limited at Wallsend as long ago as 1973 as a luxury cruise liner for the Norwegian America Line, she was sold along with her elder sister *Sagafjord* to Norwegian American Cruises in 1980. In 1983 the pair were again sold, this time to the Cunard Line, and registered in the Bahamas. Although the *Sagafjord* has since been resold for further service, the newly renamed *Caronia* represents the height of luxury. Her public rooms are described as gracious. For

The *Caronia* (1973) at the new No 2 Cruise Terminal at Dover in July 2000.

example, the split level Garden Lounge is romantically described in the marketing brochures as being bathed in natural light by day with a warm glow at night. She retains the traditional lines expected of a passenger ship and seven circuits of the teak decks of her Promenade Deck amount to one nautical mile!

Cunard's attempted take over of P&O in the early 1980s was eventually followed by the take over of Cunard itself by the construction, engineering and shipbuilding firm Kvaerner. More recently, Cunard has been resold, its ships and its brand name, to the mighty Carnival Corporation which is based at Miami. All this currently leaves the *Queen Elizabeth 2* and the *Caronia* based at Southampton, with one new build, 'Project Queen Mary 2', due in service in 2003. The current gross tonnage of the *Queen Elizabeth 2* is measured at 70,327, with accommodation for 1,778 'guests' and a crew of 921. The *Caronia* is now measured at 24,492 tons gross and has berths for 665 guests

with a crew of 376.

The complete British registered passenger fleet for 2000 is listed in Appendix 4. The average age of the ships is 15 years, the same as it was back in 1960 (see Appendix 2). Significantly, only two ships have been lost to accident at sea since World War Two, both under regrettable circumstances. These were the Royal Mail Line's *Magdelena*, on her maiden voyage, and the Booth Line's *Hildebrand*, which gave only six years service to her owners before she was lost (see Chapter 4). The British India Line's *Dara* was also lost, but as the victim of an act of terrorism (see Chapter 6). Otherwise there have been accidents and break downs, but over the last 40 years there has developed a remarkable record for safety. However, a number of British ships have been lost under tow to the breakers, including the 1948-built *Caronia* and the *Uganda*, and the safety record of many former British flag vessels has also been variable.

Princess Cruises

The company originated with the charter of the two-funnelled Canadian Pacific Railways coastal steamer *Princess Patricia*, built in 1949, and which inaugurated cruises to Alaska and Mexico's west coast in 1965. This immediate success led to the charter of the new Italian ship *Italia* which became the *Princess Italia* in time for the 1967 season. The following year the chartered *Princess Carla* joined the fleet, and in 1971 the brand new Norwegian cruise ship *Island Venture* was chartered and given the name *Island Princess*.

In 1974 the company opened discussion with P&O. Although Princess Cruises had an admirable record for marketing and designing an innovative cruise programme, they were undercapitalised and required the finance and solid support that could be provided by P&O. Once the deal had been achieved and Princess Cruises became a P&O subsidiary, the *Island Princess* was purchased outright along with her sister, the *Sea Venture*, which was renamed the *Pacific Princess*. In addition, P&O transferred their own cruise ship *Spirit of London* into the fleet as the *Sun Princess*. The *Carla* and *Italia* were then returned to their owners.

During the mid-1970s the television series *The Love Boat* was shot on board the company's ships. This was a marvellous piece of covert advertising, not only for Princess Cruises, but also for the modern cruising industry as a whole.

The first new-building for the company was the *Royal Princess*, which was delivered in 1984. This ship was innovative in that she featured a dominant outside cabin configuration and set new standards of comfort and elegance. She was followed in 1985 by the transfer of the *Sea Princess* from P&O Cruises. By 1988 the company realised that it could not simply expand by placing orders for new builds as quickly as the market would bear. As a consequence Princess Cruises purchased the Italian owned, but Los Angeles based, Sitmar Cruises, who then operated three elderly steamships and one new cruise ship. The attraction, however, was that Sitmar had orders placed for a number of new builds so that over the next five years three new 70,000 ton ships had joined the combined fleet.

The *Sea Princess* consequently only served six years in the Princess Cruises fleet before transferring back to P&O Cruises, and subsequently adopting the new name *Victoria*. Meanwhile the *Sun Princess* was sold in 1989 for further trading. During the 1990s the company grew in market position and in reputation, taking great care to provide ships with a large number of cabin balconies, with high standards of on board entertainment, and good food. The company also pride itself over the extras such as bath robes, flowers and fruit as standard cabin features. With its current modern fleet of ten cruise ships, Princess Cruises caters for about 750,000 passengers each year. The international flavour of its operations, particularly the American, Canadian and Anglo-Italian influences, are reflected in the current staffing of the ships themselves. Seven of the rapidly expanding fleet now fly the Red Ensign.

12. How the Times have Changed

Worldwide celebration of the dawn of the new millennium at the end of the 1990s was typified by the charter of the P&O cruise ship *Victoria* by the UK agents of Safmarine for a commemorative centenary voyage of the Union Castle Line. The merger of the Union Steamship Company and the Castle Packet Company had taken place in 1900. The trip was a sell out, with the *Victoria* fresh from refit and adorned in a matt finished red and black topped funnel, complete with the old Union Castle Line logo on her upper works. She slipped the quayside at Southampton on a dull, rainy and windswept December afternoon, accompanied by the fireboats whose saluting sprays soon drifted over the assembled onlookers. The 66-day voyage called at many of the old Union Castle ports, stopping at Capetown for four days to see in the

New Year, circumnavigating Africa, and arriving back at Southampton in February in time for her year 2000 world cruise.

Four of the former Union Castle passenger cargo ships are still afloat in 2000. The oldest is the former *Dunottar Castle* which was originally built in 1936 and, although much altered, survives in service as the *Princesa Victoria* with Louis Cruise Lines. The last of the line, the *Transvaal Castle* (*S A Vaal*) is also still in service as Premier Cruises' *Island Breeze*. Her immediate predecessor, the *Windsor Castle*, is lying at Eleusis in Greece with a damaged turbine unit, and at anchor nearby is the former *Amerikanis*, formerly the *Kenya Castle*. Other surviving British passenger and cargo liners are listed in Appendix 5. Of the total of 14 ships, eight are still in operational service (the former *Empress of*

The *Victoria* (1966) leaving Southampton in torrential rain on 11 December 1999, for her round-Africa Millennium cruise. She is seen wearing the funnel colours of her charterers, the Union Castle Line, whose crest adorns the stump of the forward funnel.

Canada is a regular visitor to UK ports), two are retained in static use as convention or entertainment centres, and the remainder are laid up awaiting sale or disposal for scrap.

Collectively, this rag-bag of veteran shipping represents the zenith of the British mercantile marine. The ships include the one time Blue Riband holder, the *Queen Mary*, three of the four Cunard Line intermediate passenger liners, with only the *Saxonia* (later *Carmania*) having yet gone to the ship breakers, and two of the three Canadian Pacific Line sisters, the *Empress of Britain* and *Empress of Canada*, also remaining afloat. In addition, the last two passenger mail ships built for the Union Castle Line, the *Windsor Castle* and *Transvaal Castle* also remain intact. These former passenger cargo liners are a complete contrast to the contemporary cruise ships listed in Appendix 4, although the longevity of many of them results from successful second careers in the cruise or entertainment industries.

A number of younger former British-flag cruise ships are still in use including the *Cunard Princess*, *Cunard Countess* and the *Island Princess*, the latter sold only in 1999. The contrast between the combination passenger/cargo liner (including the current *St Helena*), and the new family of cruise ships, increases as the cruise industry builds larger and more economical units. However, the pace of new building for the global cruise market barely keeps up with ever increasing demand.

The complete change of passenger shipping philosophy since the early 1960s to the present day was foreseen by Sir Basil Smallpiece in his annual statement to the Cunard shareholders in 1966:

> If we continue to regard our passenger ships only as transport vehicles for carrying people from one place to another the outlook would be grim indeed. In the field of mere transportation the aeroplanes have captured

Typical of the modern fleet of cruise ships operated under the P&O Cruises banner, is Princess Cruises' *Dawn Princess* (1997). She is seen here off Alaska.   *Princess Cruises*

129

The luxuriously appointed Passages Library aboard the *Dawn Princess* (1997).   *Princess Cruises*

The *Windsor Castle* (1960) leaving the New Docks at Southampton.

the market – ships cannot possibly compete with them either in speed or in price. But if in terms of marketing concepts we regard the passenger ship no longer simply as a means of transport, but even more as a floating resort in which people take a holiday and enjoy themselves, then the market outlook is completely changed. For instead of trading in a contracting market we shall now find ourselves in a growth industry.

How right he was, and how radical has been the change. Britain is no longer the major global passenger carrying nation – instead of the large fleet of passenger and cargo liners of the early 1960s, there is now only one passenger liner and 15 cruise ships flying the Red Ensign. The differences between the former liner voyage and the modern cruise holiday are equally radical.

The classic voyage from Southampton to the Cape, for example, illustrates the difference in passenger expectations. A Tourist Grade 4 ticket cost £167 in 1971 and, less a 5% government officer's discount, came to a princely £158 13s. In my own case, a return to Southampton, which I knew so well, to board the *SA Oranje* for her Friday lunchtime departure for Capetown, a scene I knew equally well, was an enthralling prospect. My parents had enjoyed tea in the tourist class lounge and inspected the L-shaped Bibby-type cabin as well as my cabin mate, who, it turned out, was a teacher returning to a second tour of duty in Zambia. With the visitors ashore and at precisely 1300 hours we cast off from Berth 103 to head down towards Southampton Water. I could see my parents for a long while before we changed course to clear the Royal Pier.

Shipboard life was easy and relaxed, particularly as I started on half pay from the moment I stepped aboard! Beer was 1s (5p) a pint and 2s 6d (12$\frac{1}{2}$p) got you a triple cocktail. The company was convivial and although the ship was well loaded, it was by no means

The *SA Oranje* (1948), still registered at London and crewed by Union Castle, but now owned by Safmarine, pictured in May 1968.

Ticket cover for a voyage aboard the *SA Oranje*.

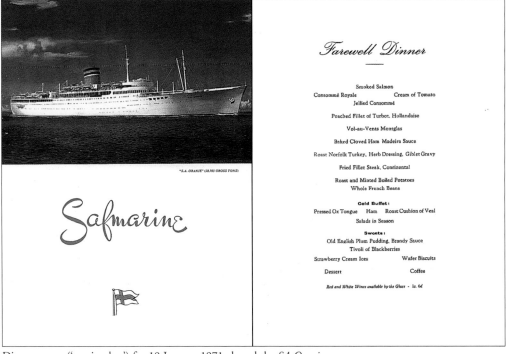

Dinner menu ('tourist class') for 19 January 1971 aboard the *SA Oranje*.

crowded. My very first overseas landfall was Las Palmas. After three days at sea we rolled down the greasy stone jetty feeling very uneasy to be on land again. Las Palmas in January was a complete contrast to Southampton, very unimpressive, but hot and steamy and full of German tourists. That night we sailed for Capetown.

On touring the Promenade Deck we found a number of palm fronds tied in a bundle, presumably ready for some first class jamboree later in the voyage. We did make a quiet forage into the posh forward end of the ship. I remember standing in silence on the foc'sle as the bows rose and dipped into the tropical night sky, and looking back towards the lights of the ship. The contrast between tourist class and first class was unabashed – we quickly scuttled aft to our place, a place where salt water baths and fresh water showers were the rule of the day!

The catering was excellent. The dining saloon offered two sittings and we were served by an army of Scouse stewards, who regaled us with nightly tales of the goings on in the 'Pig & Whistle', the crew's own bar, which was situated somewhere down near the propeller shafts! Three meals a day were the fixtures around which any other activity was pinned. Swimming was a favourite pastime, as was lounging on deck. A toddler's paddling pool was also erected under an awning, and games for the adults played half heartedly in the heat of the day. There was no other entertainment apart from an occasional recital from the ship's pianist, a film in the cinema every few nights, and what would now be described as a disco. There were what were optimistically described as ballroom dancing classes – the 'you are standing on my feet' type of ballroom dancing! The highlight of the trip was the 'Crossing the Line' ceremony, when the more gregarious took part in a time-honoured ritual played to the delight of the younger passengers. As we sailed off the West

'Crossing-the Line' ceremony in the early 1970s aboard the *Pendennis Castle* (1958).   *Jeff Davies*

Aboard the *Windsor Castle* (1960).

African coast, I smelled for the first time that glorious musty smell of a hot and humid shore. The stillness of the days was broken only by the sighting of a whale or a set of flying fish landing haplessly on the deck. All too soon we found ourselves in the Cape rollers with a dawn arrival the next day.

Many of us stayed awake that night saying our goodbyes and looking out for the mist to part over Table Mountain. The coloured family from the Cape, that I had befriended, warned that I should not even talk to them once we were in home waters. The Apartheid rules of the day meant that there were no black-skinned passengers at all, so there was no fear of us breaking that rule, at least before we disembarked. Onward travel up country was arranged by the Purser's office, and our bags were loaded for us at the quayside into a waiting covered goods wagon. I walked slowly away from the ship, now the last connection in this foreign port with my own country and my own family. I proceeded onward through the dock gates and into the busy town towards the magnificent marble-floored railway station where I boarded the Bulawayo Express, a line of steaming brown and cream carriages belonging to Rhodesia Railways. Two mornings later I found myself, a fledgling Botswana government officer, about to spend three years working in a desert, some 1,500 km from the nearest coastline.

My return voyage on a nearly deserted *Windsor Castle* three years later was a complete contrast. Gone was the sense of camaraderie and friendliness, as this was a ship under threat of withdrawal, with only a fraction of the passengers aboard that she was designed to carry. Now wiser, and a seasoned traveller, I was better able to enjoy the flesh pots of Las Palmas and this time also Madeira. Shortly after we left Madeira the swimming pool was drained, and canvas wraps were placed around the varnished hand rails to protect them from cargo handling. As we sailed into the gloom of the Western Approaches I bought my last Lion Beer in the lounge and looked forward to a well-earned rest. Sadly, all subsequent overseas tours and visits have required use of the ubiquitous Boeing 747 or one of its consorts; but I am grateful that I had the opportunity to sample the liner voyage for myself.

And how has all this changed? The publicity material describing a day in the life of P&O's 2000 cruise programme explains:

On any day of your dream cruise you could wake to a freshly-baked continental breakfast in bed, or alternatively choose to satisfy your appetite with a full English breakfast in a choice of restaurants. Afterwards there's an opportunity for a light workout in the gym perhaps, a refreshing dip in a jacuzzi, or a visit to the beauty therapists. Next, why not settle back and work on your tan in your favourite corner of the sundeck?

The description continues through lunch and the busy afternoon, and ends:

But the evening is only just beginning. There are casinos to tempt you, pubs and bars to relax in and new-found friends to meet up with for cocktails. Take in one of the glamorous West-End style floorshows, or promenade under the stars before a night-cap and if the mood grabs you, dance until dawn in the nightclub.

Perhaps the most interesting contrast with the liner voyage is that there is no mention of any destination – the brochure is not trying to sell the Mediterranean, the Caribbean or the Norwegian fjords, but is selling cruising, P&O style.

The ports that served the passenger ships have also changed. Southampton remains the home of Cunard and P&O, but Princess Cruises prefer the new cruise port facilities at Dover as their UK base, although they have used both Tilbury and Southampton in the past. Harwich is also increasingly used as a cruise ship terminal. The *St Helena*, the last of the passenger-cargo liners, is based at Cardiff. But at Liverpool and Glasgow, London and Hull, and at Rotterdam, Le Havre, Cherbourg and Cobh, there are no Ellerman liners loading for Africa or Blue Funnel gods and goddesses preparing for another voyage to the East. Today the passengers travel by air, and the cargo by container ship.

All this is a far cry to the description of the delivery of the mails in the 1920s:

At some of the West Indian islands where the Royal Mail Steam Packet Company delivers the mails, the waterproof packet containing the letters and papers is enclosed in a water-tight barrel, which is securely attached to a small raft bearing a staff with a weight at one end so that it will float upright, and the Company's flag at the end above the water. When all is ready, this is thrown overboard, but not before a boat is seen coming from the shore to pick it up.

Today, Glasgow has an Armadillo exhibition and hotel complex, Liverpool a marina and maritime museum, Southampton an oceanographic centre, and London, the Canary Wharf. But there are no liners in the docks. How the times have changed.

Appendix 1

British ships, with accommodation for more than 12 passengers, in service between 1960 and 2000

Anchor Line
To Karachi and Bombay, via Port Said, Aden and Port Sudan

Name	Year	GRT	Speed (knots)	Passengers	Company service	Wdn
Circassia	1937	11,170	16	298	1937–66	1966
Cilicia	1938	11,172	16	298	1938–66	1980
Caledonia	1948	11,255	16	304	1948–66	1971

Bibby Line (Bibby Brothers & Company Limited)
To Port Said, Port Sudan, Aden, Colombo and Rangoon, trooping

Name	Year	GRT	Speed (knots)	Passengers	Company service	Wdn
Worcestershire	1931	10,392	14	115	1931–61	1961
Derbyshire	1935	10,641	14	115	1935–64	1964
*Devonshire**	1939	12,773	13	1,149	1939–62	1967
Warwickshire	1948	8,917	14	76	1948–65	1980
Leicestershire	1949	8,912	14	76	1949–64	1966
*Oxfordshire**	1957	20,586	17	1,500	1957–62	–

*Troopship

Blue Funnel Line (Alfred Holt & Company; includes Ocean Steamship Company Limited and China Mutual Steam Navigation Company)
To Australia via South Africa, and to Malaya, Philippines, China and Japan. Also Singapore to Australia and Indonesia to Jeddah.

Name	Year	GRT	Speed (knots)	Passengers	Company service	Wdn
Gorgon	1933	3,678	13	72	1933–64	1964
Charon	1936	3,964	13	88	1936–64	1964
Gunung Djati	1936	17,891	16	2,100+	1958–62	1987
Helenus	1949	10,129	18	30	1949–72	1972
Peleus	1949	10,093	18	30	1949–72	1972
Pyrrhus	1949	10,093	18	30	1949–72	1972
Hector	1950	10,125	18	30	1950–72	1972
Jason	1950	10,160	18	30	1950–72	1972
Patroclus	1950	10,109	18	30	1950–73	1973
Perseus	1950	10,109	18	30	1950–73	1973
Ixion	1951	10,125	18	30	1951–72	1972
Centaur	1963	8,262	20	190	1964–84*	–

*Re-registered at Singapore in 1973

Blue Star Line
Via Lisbon and the Canary Islands to Rio de Janeiro, Santos, Montevideo and Buenos Aires

Name	Year	GRT	Speed (knots)	Passengers	Company service	Wdn
Argentina Star	1947	10,716	16	51	1947–72	1972
Brazil Star	1947	10,722	16	53	1947–72	1972
Paraguay Star	1948	10,723	16	53	1947–69	1969

Name	Year	GRT	Speed (knots)	Passengers	Company service	Wdn
Uruguay Star	1948	10,722	16	53	1948–72	1972
Iberia Star	1950	10,854	16	228	1963–65	1973

Booth Line
To the Amazon as far as Manaos, via Lisbon and Madeira and the Caribbean

Name	Year	GRT	Speed (knots)	Passengers	Company service	Wdn
Anselm	1950	10,950	16	228	1961–63	1973
Hubert	1955	8,062	15	170	1955–65	1984

British India Line (British India Steam Navigation Company)
Indian Ocean services connecting the Far East with Africa and the Middle East, trooping, cruises

Name	Year	GRT	Speed (knots)	Passengers	Company service	Wdn
Rajula	1926	8,496	12	1,770	1926–73	1975
*Dilwara**	1936	12,555	14	1,254	1936–60	1971
Dunera	1937	12,615	14	1,020	1937–67	1967
Amra	1938	8,314	16	959	1938–66	1966
Devonia	1939	12,796	13	1,030	1962–67	1967
Aronda	1941	8,396	16	1,950	1941–63	1963
Dumra	1946	4,867	14	1,150	1946–78	1979
Dwarka	1947	4,851	13	1,100	1947–61	1982
Kampala	1947	10,304	16	1,065	1947–71	1971
Sangola	1947	8,647	14	1,415	1947–62	1963
Sirdhana	1947	8,608	14	1,400	1947–72	1972
Dara	1948	5,030	14	1,030	1948–61	1961
Karanja	1948	10,294	16	1,065	1948–76	1989
Daressa	1950	4,180	13	586	1950–64	1974
Mombasa	1950	2,213	12	274	1950–61	1973
Santhia	1950	8,908	14	1,193	1950–67	1977
Kenya	1951	14,464	16	297	1951–69	1969
Uganda	1952	14,430	16	300	1952–86	1986
Nevasa	1956	20,527	17	1,500	1956–75	1975

*Troopship

Canadian Pacific Steamships Limited
To Quebec and Montreal in summer, and St John in winter, cruises

Name	Year	GRT	Speed (knots)	Passengers	Company service	Wdn
Empress of France	1928	20,448	18	700	1928–60	1960
Empress of Britain	1956	25,516	20	1,054	1956–65	–
Empress of England	1957	25,585	20	1,058	1957–70	1975
Empress of Canada	1961	27,284	20	1,056	1961–72	–

Cunard Line (Cunard Steamship Company Limited)
To New York, Quebec and Montreal (summer) and Halifax (winter), also cruises

Name	Year	GRT	Speed (knots)	Passengers	Company service	Wdn
Britannic	1930	27,666	18	993	1934–60	1960
Queen Mary	1936	81,237	28	1,995	1936–67	–
Mauretania	1939	35,655	23	1,140	1939–65	1965
Queen Elizabeth	1940	83,637	28	2,283	1940–70	1972

Name	Year	GRT	Speed (knots)	Passengers	Company service	Wdn
Media	1947	13,345	18	250	1947–61	1989
Parthia	1948	34,172	22	932	1948–68	1974
Caronia	1948	13,362	18	250	1948–61	1970
Saxonia/Carmania	1954	21,637	19	925	1954–73	–
Ivernia/Franconia	1955	21,717	19	925	1955–73	–
Carinthia	1956	21,947	19	869	1956–68	–
Sylvania	1957	21,989	19	869	1957–68	–
Queen Elizabeth 2	1969	65,863	28	2,005	1969–	–
Cunard Adventurer	1971	14,155	20	806	1971–76	–
Cunard Ambassador	1972	14,155	20	806	1972–75	1985
Caronia	1973	24,492	20	665	2000–*	–
Cunard Countess	1976	17,495	20	750	1976–95	–
Cunard Princess	1977	17,495	20	750	1977–80**	–
*Sea Goddess I****	1984	4,253	15	116	1998–99	–
*Sea Goddess II****	1985	4,253	15	116	1998–99	–

*transferred from Bahamas registry 2000
**transferred to Bahamas registry 1980
***temporally registered in the Isle of Man

Curnow Shipping Limited
To St Helena and Capetown

Name	Year	GRT	Speed (knots)	Passengers	Company service	Wdn
St Helena	1963	3,150	16	88	1977–90	–
St Helena	1990	6,767	17	132	1990–	–

Donaldson Line (Donaldson Brothers & Black Limited)
To Montreal (summer) and St John or Pacific Coast ports (winter)

Name	Year	GRT	Speed (knots)	Passengers	Company service	Wdn
Laurentia	1945	8,323	15	55	1946–67	1967
Lismoria	1945	8,349	15	55	1946–67	1967

Elder Dempster Lines
To Freetown, Takoradi and Lagos via Las Palmas

Name	Year	GRT	Speed (knots)	Passengers	Company service	Wdn
Calabar	1936	8,305	13	105	1957–63	1963
Winneba	1938	8,355	13	105	1957–63	1963
Tarkwa	1944	7,414	13	72	1944–66	1971
Tamele	1945	7,173	13	36	1944–66	1973
Accra	1947	11,644	15	273	1947–67	1967
Apapa	1948	11,651	15	273	1948–68	1975
Aureol	1951	14,083	16	353	1951–74	–

Elders & Fyffes Limited
To the West Indies

Name	Year	GRT	Speed (knots)	Passengers	Company service	Wdn
Golfito	1949	8,740	17	111	1949–71	1971
Camito	1956	8,687	17	113	1956–73	1973

Ellerman & Bucknall Lines
To southern African ports

Name	Year	GRT	Speed (knots)	Passengers	Company service	Wdn
City of Port Elizabeth	1952	13,363	16	107	1952–71	1980
City of Exeter	1953	13,345	16	107	1953–71	–
City of York	1953	13,345	16	107	1953–71	–
City of Durban	1954	13,345	16	107	1954–71	1974

Furness Bermuda Line
New York to Bermuda, cruises

Name	Year	GRT	Speed (knots)	Passengers	Company service	Wdn
Queen of Bermuda	1933	22,501	20	733	1933–66	1966
Ocean Monarch	1951	13,654	18	440	1951–67	1981

Furness Warren Line
To Halifax and St Johns

Name	Year	GRT	Speed (knots)	Passengers	Company service	Wdn
Nova Scotia	1947	7,438	15	154	1947–62	1971
Newfoundland	1948	7,437	15	154	1948–62	1971

Glen Line (Glen & Shire Line)
To the Far East

Name	Year	GRT	Speed (knots)	Passengers	Company service	Wdn
Denbighshire	1938	8,983	17	18	1938–68	1969
Glenearn	1938	8,960	17	18	1938–71	1971
Glenroy	1938	8,959	17	18	1938–66	1966
Glengyle	1939	8,957	17	18	1939–70	1971
Glenartney	1940	8,992	17	18	1940–67	1967
Glengarry	1940	9,144	17	18	1946–70	1971
Glenorchy	1941	9,324	17	18	1948–70	1971
Breconshire	1942	9,061	17	18	1946–67	1967

Hebridean Island Cruises Limited
Cruises

Name	Year	GRT	Speed (knots)	Passengers	Company service	Wdn
Hebridean Princess	1964	2,112	14	49	1989–	–
Hebridean Spirit	1991	4,200	15	79	2000–	–

Henderson Line (P. Henderson & Company, British & Burmese Steam Navigation Company)
To Rangoon via Port Said, Port Sudan and Aden

Name	Year	GRT	Speed (knots)	Passengers	Company service	Wdn
Prome	1937	7,043	14	76	1937–62	1962
Salween	1938	7,063	14	74	1938–62	1962

Ministry of Transport (under Donaldson Line management)
To New Zealand

Name	Year	GRT	Speed (knots)	Passengers	Company service	Wdn
Captain Cook	1925	13,867	15	950	1951–60	1960
*Empire Fowey**	1936	19,047	20	1,000	1945–60	1960

*Troopship

New Zealand Shipping Company Limited
To New Zealand via Panama

Name	Year	GRT	Speed (knots)	Passengers	Company service	Wdn
Rangitata	1929	16,969	16	123	1929–62	1962
Rangitiki	1929	16,985	16	121	1929–62	1962
Remuera	1948	13,619	18	350	1961–64	1970
Rangitane	1949	21,867	17	436	1949–68	1976
Rangitoto	1949	21,809	17	436	1949–69	1976
Ruahine	1951	17,851	17	267	1951–68	1974

Pacific Steam Navigation Company
Via West Indies to Pacific coast South American ports

Name	Year	GRT	Speed (knots)	Passengers	Company service	Wdn
Reina del Mar	1956	20,334	18	766	1956–64	1975

Peninsular and Oriental Steam Navigation Company (incorporating the Orient Line)
To Australia and the Far East and west coast Canada and America, cruises

Name	Year	GRT	Speed (knots)	Passengers	Company service	Wdn
Orontes	1929	20,186	18	1,370	1929–62	1962
Carthage	1931	14,280	17	394	1931–61	1961
Corfu	1931	14,280	17	394	1931–61	1961
Strathnaver	1931	22,270	19	1,069	1931–62	1962
Strathaird	1932	22,568	19	1,069	1932–61	1961
Orion	1935	23,696	19	1,406	1935–63	1963
Strathmore	1935	23,580	19	984	1935–63	1969
Stratheden	1937	23,732	19	980	1937–64	1969
Canton	1938	16,033	18	542	1938–62	1962
Orcades	1948	28,164	22	1,365	1948–73	1973
Himalaya	1949	27,955	22	1,159	1949–74	1974
Chusan	1950	24,215	22	1,026	1950–73	1973
Oronsay	1951	27,632	22	1,416	1951–75	1975
Arcadia	1954	29,734	22	1,390	1954–79	1979
Iberia	1954	29,614	22	1,406	1954–72	1972
Orsova	1954	28,790	22	1,503	1954–73	1973
Chitral	1956	13,724	16	240	1961–70	1976
Cathay	1957	13,809	16	240	1961–69	–
Oriana	1960	41,923	27	2,134	1960–86	–
Canberra	1961	45,270	27	2,272	1961–98	1998
Sea Princess/Victoria	1966	27,670	21	750	1978–	–
Spirit of London	1972	17,370	20	742	1972–74	–
Arcadia	1989	63,524	22	1,531	1997–	–
Oriana	1998	69,153	24	1,928	1998–	–
Aurora	2000	76,000	24	1,950	2000–	–

P&O Australia
Cruises

Name	Year	GRT	Speed (knots)	Passengers	Company service	Wdn
Pacific Sky	1984	46,314	19	1,200	2000–	–

Princess Cruises
Cruises

Name	Year	GRT	Speed (knots)	Passengers	Company service	Wdn
Pacific Princess	1971	19,904	20	646	1974–	–
Island Princess	1972	19,907	20	646	1972–99	–
Sun Princess	1972	17,370	20	742	1974–88	–
Royal Princess	1984	44,348	22	1,200	1984–	–
Sky Princess	1984	46,314	19	1,200	1984–2000	–
Regal Princess	1991	69,845	22	1,590	1991–	–
Sun Princess	1995	77,441	21	1,950	1995–	–
Dawn Princess	1997	77,441	21	1,950	1997–	–
Sea Princess	1998	77,441	21	1,950	1998–	–
Ocean Princess	2000	77,441	21	1,950	2000–	–

Royal Mail Lines Limited
To South America Atlantic coast, cruises

Name	Year	GRT	Speed (knots)	Passengers	Company service	Wdn
Andes	1939	26,860	21	500	1939–71	1971
Amazon	1959	20,348	17	449	1959–68	1981
Aragon	1960	20,362	17	449	1960–69	1981
Arlanza	1960	20,362	17	449	1960–68	1981

Shaw Savill Line (Shaw Savill & Albion Company Limited)
To Australia and New Zealand, round-the-world, cruises

Name	Year	GRT	Speed (knots)	Passengers	Company service	Wdn
Dominion Monarch	1939	26,463	20	508	1939–62	1962
Athenic	1947	15,182	17	85	1947–69	1969
Corinthic	1947	15,682	17	85	1947–69	1969
Ceramic	1948	15,896	17	85	1948–72	1972
Gothic	1948	15,902	17	85	1948–69	1969
Southern Cross	1955	20,204	20	1,100	1955–73	–
Ocean Monarch	1957	25,971	20	1,372	1970–75	1975
Akaroa	1959	20,348	17	470	1968–71	1981
Aranda	1960	20,362	17	470	1969–71	1981
Arawa	1960	20,362	17	470	1968–71	1981
Northern Star	1962	24,731	20	1,437	1962–76	1976

Union Castle Line (Union-Mail Steamship Company)
To South Africa via Las Palmas, to East Africa via Suez, round Africa, cruises

Name	Year	GRT	Speed (knots)	Passengers	Company service	Wdn
Carnarvon Castle	1926	20,148	20	584	1926–62	1962
Winchester Castle	1930	20,001	20	587	1930–60	1960
Athlone Castle	1936	25,567	20	783	1936–65	1965
Stirling Castle	1936	25,554	20	783	1936–66	1966
Capetown Castle	1938	27,002	20	796	1938–67	1967
Durban Castle	1938	17,382	18	539	1938–62	1962
Warwick Castle	1939	17,387	18	539	1938–62*	1962

*As *Pretoria Castle*, sold to the Admiralty in 1942, repurchased 1946.

Name	Year	GRT	Speed (knots)	Passengers	Company service	Wdn
Pretoria Castle/ SA Oranje	1948	28,705	22	755	1948–69	1975
Edinburgh Castle	1948	28,705	22	755	1948–76	1976
Rhodesia Castle	1951	17,041	17	552	1951–67	1967
Braemar Castle	1952	17,029	17	552	1952–65	1965
Kenya Castle	1952	17,041	17	526	1952–67	–
Reina del Mar	1956	20,501	18	998	1964–75	1975
Pendennis Castle	1958	28,582	22	736	1958–76	1980
Windsor Castle	1960	37,640	23	822	1960–77	–
Transvaal Castle/ SA Vaal	1961	32,697	23	763	1961–69	–

Appendix 2

British liners with more than 50 passenger berths in service in 1960. (Ship names in normal type indicate additional deck or bunk capacity.)

Ship	Year	GRT	1st class	2/3 class	Company
Accra	1947	11,600	259	24	Elder Dempster Lines
Amazon	1960	20,348	92	357	Royal Mail Lines Ltd
Amra	1938	8,214	0	959	British India Line
Andes	1939	25,676	500	0	Royal Mail Lines Ltd
Apapa	1948	11,607	259	24	Elder Dempster Lines
Aragon	1960	20,362	92	357	Royal Mail Lines Ltd
Arcadia	1954	29,734	655	735	P&O
Argentina Star	1947	10,716	51	0	Blue Star Line
Arlanza	1960	20,352	92	357	Royal Mail Lines Ltd
Aronda	1941	8,396	44	110	British India Line
Athenic	1947	15,182	85	0	Shaw Savill Line
Athlone Castle	1936	25,567	245	538	Union Castle Line
Aureol	1951	14,083	253	100	Elder Dempster Lines
Braemar Castle	1952	17,029	0	552	Union Castle Line
Brazil Star	1947	10,716	53	0	Blue Star Line
Britannic	1930	27,666	429	564	Cunard Line
Calabar	1936	8,305	105	0	Elder Dempster Lines
Caledonia	1948	11,252	304	0	Anchor Line
Camito	1956	8,687	113	0	Elders & Fyffes Ltd
Canton	1938	16,033	298	244	P&O
Capetown Castle	1938	27,002	243	553	Union Castle Line
Captain Cook	1925	13,807	0	950	Ministry of Transport
Carinthia	1956	21,947	125	800	Cunard Line
Carnarvon Castle	1926	20,141	134	450	Union Castle Line
Caronia	1948	34,183	581	351	Cunard Line
Carthage	1931	14,238	181	213	P&O
Ceramic	1948	15,896	85	0	Shaw Savill Line
Charon	1936	3,964	88	0	Blue Funnel Line
Chusan	1950	24,215	475	551	P&O
Cilicia	1938	11,157	298	0	Anchor Line
Circassia	1937	11,170	298	0	Anchor Line
City of Durban	1954	13,345	107	0	Ellerman & Bucknall Lines
City of Exeter	1953	13,345	107	0	Ellerman & Bucknall Lines
City of Port Elizabeth	1952	13,363	107	0	Ellerman & Bucknall Lines
City of York	1953	13,345	107	0	Ellerman & Bucknall Lines
Corfu	1931	14,280	181	213	P&O
Corinthic	1947	15,682	85	0	Shaw Savill Line
Dara	1948	5,030	13	65	British India Line
Daressa	1950	5,180	26	60	British India Line
Derbyshire	1935	10,623	115	0	Bibby Line
*Devonshire**	1939	11,275	130	195	Bibby Line

Ship	Year	GRT	1st class	2/3 class	Company
*Dilwara**	1936	12,555	125	195	British India Line
Dominion Monarch	1939	26,463	508	0	Shaw Savill Line
Dumra	1946	4,867	13	41	British India Line
*Dunera**	1937	12,615	123	195	British India Line
Durban Castle	1938	17,382	180	359	Union Castle Line
Dwarka	1947	4,851	13	41	British India Line
Edinburgh Castle	1948	28,705	214	541	Union Castle Line
*Empire Fowey**	1936	19,047	–	–	Ministry of Transport
Empress of Britain	1956	25,516	160	894	Can. Pacific Steamships Ltd
Empress of England	1957	25,585	160	898	Can. Pacific Steamships Ltd
Empress of France	1928	20,448	218	482	Can. Pacific Steamships Ltd
Golfito	1949	8,736	111	0	Elders & Fyffes Ltd
Gorgon	1933	3,678	72	0	Blue Funnel Line
Gothic	1948	15,902	85	0	Shaw Savill Line
Gunung Djati	1936	18,036	106	2,000	Blue Funnel Line
Himalaya	1949	27,955	758	401	P&O
Hubert	1955	7,905	74	96	Booth Line
Iberia	1954	29,614	673	733	P&O
Ivernia	1955	21,717	125	800	Cunard Line
Kampala	1947	10,304	60	1,005	British India Line
Karanja	1948	10,294	60	1,005	British India Line
Kenya	1951	14,434	194	103	British India Line
Kenya Castle	1952	17,041	0	526	Union Castle Line
Laurentia	1945	8,249	55	0	Donaldson Line
Leicestershire	1949	8,908	76	0	Bibby Line
Lismoria	1945	8,323	55	0	Donaldson Line
Mauretania	1939	35,677	470	670	Cunard Line
Media	1947	13,345	250	0	Cunard Line
*Nevasa**	1956	20,527	220	280	British India Line
Newfoundland	1948	7,437	62	92	Johnston Warren Lines
Nova Scotia	1947	7,438	62	92	Johnston Warren Lines
Ocean Monarch	1951	13,654	440	0	Furness Withy & Co
Orcades	1949	28,164	631	734	Orient Line
Oriana	1960	41,923	638	1,496	Orient Line
Orion	1935	23,696	0	1,406	Orient Line
Oronsay	1951	27,632	612	804	Orient Line
Orontes	1929	20,186	0	1,370	Orient Line
Orsova	1954	28,790	694	809	Orient Line
*Oxfordshire**	1956	20,568	220	280	Bibby Line
Paraguay Star	1948	10,722	53	0	Blue Star Line
Parthia	1948	13,362	250	0	Cunard Line
Pendennis Castle	1958	28,582	197	473	Union Castle Line
Pretoria Castle	1948	28,705	214	541	Union Castle Line
Prome	1937	7,043	76	0	Henderson Line
Queen Elizabeth	1940	83,673	823	1,400	Cunard Line
Queen Mary	1936	81,237	711	1,284	Cunard Line
Queen of Bermuda	1933	22,501	733	0	Furness Withy & Co
Rajula	1926	8,496	37	133	British India Line
Rangitane	1949	21,867	0	436	New Zealand Line

Ship	Year	GRT	1st class	2/3 class	Company
Rangitata	1929	16,969	123	288	New Zealand Line
Rangitiki	1929	16,984	121	284	New Zealand Line
Rangitoto	1949	21,809	0	436	New Zealand Line
Reina del Mar	1956	20,225	207	559	Pacific Line
Rhodesia Castle	1951	17,041	0	552	Union Castle Line
Ruahine	1951	17,851	0	267	New Zealand Line
Salween	1938	7,063	74	0	Henderson Line
Sangola	1947	8,646	21	34	British India Line
Santhia	1950	8,908	25	416	British India Line
Saxonia	1954	21,637	125	800	Cunard Line
Sirdhana	1947	8,608	21	32	British India Line
Southern Cross	1955	20,203	0	1,100	Shaw Savill Line
Stirling Castle	1936	25,554	245	538	Union Castle Line
Strathaird	1932	22,568	0	1,242	P&O
Stratheden	1937	23,732	527	453	P&O
Strathmore	1935	23,580	497	487	P&O
Strathnaver	1931	22,270	0	1,252	P&O
Sylvania	1957	21,989	125	800	Cunard Line
Tamele	1945	7,172	40	36	Elder Dempster Lines
Tarkwa	1944	7,416	40	32	Elder Dempster Lines
Uganda	1952	14,430	167	133	British India Line
Uruguay Star	1948	10,723	53	0	Blue Star Line
Warwick Castle	1938	17,387	180	359	Union Castle Line
Warwickshire	1948	8,903	76	0	Bibby Line
Winchester Castle	1930	2,001	189	398	Union Castle Line
Windsor Castle	1960	37,640	237	585	Union Castle Line
Winneba	1938	8,355	105	0	Elder Dempster Lines
Worcestershire	1931	10,319	115	0	Bibby Line

*Troopship

Appendix 3

The three *Queens*

	Queen Mary	Queen Elizabeth	Queen Elizabeth 2
Completed	1936	1939	1968
Gross tonnage	81,237	83,637	65,863
Length (m)	311	314	294
Beam (m)	36	36	32
Height (m)*	38	40	41
Maximum draught (m)	12.0	12.0	9.9
Passenger capacity	1,948	2,082	2,025
No. of boilers	27[1]	12[1]	3[2]
No. of propellers	4	4	2
Swimming pools	2 indoor	2 indoor, 1 outdoor	2 indoor, 2 outdoor
No. of lifts	20	24	22

*Height from keel to base of funnel.

[1] Single reduction geared turbines, 120,000 shaft kW.

[2] Double reduction geared turbines, 82,000 shaft kW.

Appendix 4

British liners and cruise ships in service in 2000

Ship	Year	GRT	Passengers	Company
Caronia	1973	24,492	665	Cunard Line
Queen Elizabeth 2	1968	70,327	1,778	Cunard Line
Oriana	1995	69,153	1,928	P&O
Victoria	1966	28,891	782	P&O
Arcadia	1989	63,524	1,531	P&O
Aurora	2000	76,000	1,975	P&O
Pacific Sky	1984	46,314	1,200	P&O Australia
Pacific Princess	1971	20,186	610	Princess Cruises
Royal Princess	1984	44,588	1,200	Princess Cruises
Regal Princess	1991	69,845	1,590	Princess Cruises
Sun Princess	1995	77,441	1,950	Princess Cruises
Dawn Princess	1997	77,441	1,950	Princess Cruises
Sea Princess	1998	77,441	1,950	Princess Cruises
Ocean Princess	2000	77,441	1,950	Princess Cruises
Hebridean Princess	1964	2,112	49	Hebridean Island Cruises
*Hebridean Spirit**	1991	4,200	79	Hebridean Island Cruises
St Helena	1990	6,767	132	Curnow Shipping Company

* Commenced service in July 2001. Was originally built as the *Renaissance VI* and latterly named the *Megastar Capricorn*.

Appendix 5

Former British passenger liners still afloat in 2000

Former name	Year	Current name	Current use
Dunnottar Castle *	1936	*Princesa Victoria*	In use: owners Louis Cruise Lines
Queen Mary	1936		Static role, Long Beach, California
Aureol **	1951	*Marianna VI*	Lying at Eleusis
Kenya Castle	1952	*Amerikanis*	Lying at Eleusis
City of York	1953	*Mediterranean Sky*	Lying at Eleusis
Ivernia/Franconia	1955	*Fedor Shalyapin*	Lying at Ilsychevsk
Southern Cross	1955	*Ocean Breeze*	In use: owners Dolphin Cruise Lines
Carinthia	1956	*China Sea Discovery*	In use: owners Allegiance Capital Corp
Empress Of Britain	1956	*Topaz*	In use: owners Topaz International
Sylvania	1957	*Albatross*	In use: owners Phoenix Seereisen
Oriana	1960		Static role, Shanghai
Windsor Castle	1960	*Margarita L*	Lying at Eleusis
Empress of Canada	1961	*Apollon*	In use: owners Epirotiki Line
Transvaal Castle	1961	*Island Breeze*	In use: owners Premier Cruises
Centaur	1963	*Hai Da*	In use: owners China Shipping Co

*Sold out of the Union Castle fleet in 1958.
**Aureol* was sold for demolition in 2001.

Bibliography

Periodicals
Marine Propulsion International
Sea Breezes
Ships Monthly

Books

Eriksen, R, *St Helena lifeline*, Mallett & Bell Publications, 1994

Hodson, N, *The race to the Cape, a story of the Union Castle Line 1857-1977*, Navigator Books, 1995

Howarth, D, and Howarth, S, *The story of P&O, the Peninsular and Oriental Steam Navigation Company*, Weidenfeld & Nicolson, 1986

Laird, D, *Paddy Henderson*, George Outram & Co Ltd, 1961

Miller, W, *British ocean liners, a twilight era, 1960-85*, Patrick Stephens, 1986

Roskill, SW, *A merchant fleet at war, Alfred Holt & Co 1939-1945*, Collins, 1962

Talbot-Booth, EC, *Merchant ships 1963 edition. The Journal of Commerce and Shipping Telegraph*, 1963

Index

British registered vessels are in plain type; other nationalities are in italics. Ship names will be followed by a year in parentheses. Numbers in italics indicate an illustration of, or relating to, the subject matter.